We the People

THE CONSTITUTION IN AMERICAN LIFE

Banner of the Society of Pewterers, carried in the Federal Procession of 1788 in New York.
The New-York Historical Society

We the People

THE CONSTITUTION IN AMERICAN LIFE

Robert S. Peck

Harry N. Abrams, Inc., Publishers, New York
in cooperation with
KQED, Inc., and The American Bar Association

Editor: Adele Westbrook

Designer: Doris Leath

Photo Research: Eric Himmel and Pamela Bass

Cover Photography: George Hein

Library of Congress Cataloging-in-Publication Data

Peck, Robert S.
We the people.

Bibliography: p.
Includes index.
1. United States—Constitutional law. 2. United States—Constitutional history. I. KQED-TV (Television station: San Francisco, Calif.) II. American Bar Association. III. Title.
KF4550.Z9P43 1987 342.73'029 86–32215
ISBN 0–8109–1789–0 347.30229

The opinions expressed in this book do not necessarily represent the specific positions of the management of the American Bar Association, or Merrill Lynch & Co., Inc., or KQED, Inc.

Published in 1987 by Harry N. Abrams, Incorporated, New York

Times Mirror Books

Printed and bound in the United States of America

Contents

Acknowledgments

In 1982, a San Francisco television producer and a lawyer in Chicago began independently to develop the ideas that would become "We The People." The two joined forces a year later, and for almost four years Beverly J. Ornstein, executive producer for "We The People" at public broadcasting station KQED, Inc., and Robert S. Peck of the American Bar Association labored to develop a television series and a book to enhance Americans' understanding of the Constitution of the United States of America and its enduring significance in our society.

Initial support for "We The People" came in the form of research and development grants from the National Endowment for the Humanities. Primary funding for the program was provided by KQED and the ABA during the early stages of actual development.

Since its founding in 1954, KQED in San Francisco has had an exceptional history as a leading producer of news and public affairs programs, exploring the most crucial and difficult issues of our times.

The American Bar Association, more than 330,000 members strong, is the world's largest voluntary professional organization. Its members include the country's leading lawyers, legal scholars, and jurists. Public understanding about the law and legal system is one of the ABA's highest priorities, leading the Association to commit its resources during the Bicentennial period to raising public appreciation of the Constitution and its role in American life through "We The People."

The successful completion of "We The People" was assured in the summer of 1986, when Merrill Lynch & Co., Inc., joined the endeavor as the major corporate underwriter.

Merrill Lynch, one of the world's largest financial services firms, has a long tradition of support for educational, cultural, and civic activities. Its sponsorship of "We The People" is part of the firm's national program to commemorate the Bicentennial of the Constitution of the United States of America and its ratification by the states.

"We The People" represents the efforts of the aforementioned individuals and organizations, as well as the contributions of many others. It has benefited from the counsel and ideas of the production staff of the "We The People" television series, the committee members and staff of the ABA's Public Education Division, and a distinguished board of advisors.

And so, on the occasion of the 200th anniversary of the Constitution, KQED, the American Bar Association, and Merrill Lynch are proud to honor the document that protects individual liberties and the American way of life.

UNCLE SAM. "Whe-ew!! And what will the tew hundredth be?"

Introduction

Adaptation of an 1889 cartoon, origin unknown. Division of Political History, Smithsonian Institution, Washington, D.C. Courtesy Project '87, Washington, D.C.

Writing a book or producing a television series about the United States Constitution is a daunting task—especially when there is the added significance of being part of a two-hundredth anniversary celebration. The challenge is to convey universally exalted concepts in clear and eloquent terms. It is obviously difficult to do even minimal justice to the vital concepts and illuminating history that must be woven together in all too few pages, and there is always the danger of according scant attention to points some will regard as being critical. Still, you plunge ahead, because the Constitution of the United States of America is something very special, and its two-hundredth anniversary a time for both celebration and reflection.

It is natural for Americans to marvel at their Constitution. Its longevity alone would be reason enough to rejoice; no other written national constitution can match it. Old age, however, is not sufficient reason for celebration unless it represents—as it does here—a set of fundamental principles that the diverse members of our pluralistic society can support. The Constitution's emphasis on human dignity is embodied in the guarantee of individual liberty. That guarantee, more than any of this nation's many other blessings, has provided the connective tissue

Poster for the Sesquicentennial of the Constitution by Howard Chandler Christy. National Archives. Courtesy Project '87, Washington, D.C.

The words spoken at the Philadelphia Convention are cited to resolve issues the Framers never contemplated. Independence Hall, Philadelphia, Pennsylvania. Essex Institute, Salem, Massachusetts

that unifies those who trace their heritage back to the Mayflower with the most recent immigrants to this land.

We rely upon the Constitution for many things. We search its phrases for the answer to every public question, from the most minor to the most momentous. In every policy debate, both sides are apt to invoke the Constitution in support of their cause. This characteristic of American politics underscores that document's standing as a guide to a very modern American way of life. The Constitution is not just ancient parchment to be venerated without further reflection, but a system that encourages introspection. Its counterintuitive nature prevents us from taking an expedient detour, simply because a temporary majority points that way. Instead, it encourages us to discover the larger public interest—one that manifests itself only over longer periods of time. Thus, it provides a process that, to the extent any process can, induces us to choose wisely in making public-policy decisions. The Constitution's very nature impels us to think through the choices we are permitted to make and the possible ramifications of those choices. It gives voice to even the most politically powerless so that the unintended, potentially hazardous effects of our societal choices may be recognized and corrected—provided that we are willing to steer clear of the shoals of our own creation.

The most interesting aspect of the constitutional process is that it is comprised of certain guidelines and guarantees that inform our actions as a nation and are intended to ensure liberty by making it difficult for the government to act against the interests of the people. Rather than anticipate every decision government must make, the Constitution provides broad policy discretion within a framework sensitive to individual rights.

That sensitivity is inherent in a structure that constitutes a government of limited powers and provides a system of checks and balances to prevent rash or oppressive acts. It is inherent in a Bill of Rights that guarantees freedom from governmental interference in areas vital to a system of individual liberty. It is inherent in a system that recognizes minority interests must be protected from the whims and passions of fleeting political majorities. Our fourth president, the man most often referred to as the "Father of the Constitution," James Madison, described it well:

> The prescriptions in favor of liberty ought to be levelled against that quarter where the greatest danger lies, namely, that which possesses the highest prerogative of power. But this is not found in either the Executive or Legislative departments of Government, but in the body of the people, operating by the majority against the minority.

There is no substitute for popular wisdom. Not a single constitutional guarantee can survive a people bent upon their own destruction. Some of the finest hours in our history have occurred when the protections in the document have been successfully asserted to vindicate constitutional values against majority impulses; many of its worst moments have occurred when those attempts have failed. More than 150 years ago, in *Democracy in America*, Alexis de Tocqueville recognized how important it is for the people to assume responsibility for the tasks self-government requires of the citizenry. "The majority in the United States," he wrote, "has immense actual power and a power of opinion which is almost as great. When once its mind is made up on any question, there are, so to say, no obstacles which can retard, much less halt its progress and give it time to hear the wails of those it crushes as it passes."

This observation reveals an important truism that is missing from the usual analysis of the constitutional system. Decisions of a constitutional dimension are not just made in the corridors of power in Washington, D.C., although obviously, many of the most visible constitutional questions are decided there. Nevertheless, more decisions—decisions that do not necessarily make headlines—are made by the people: when they vote, when they reach a community consensus on a local question, when they choose to read a particular book or news-

James Madison by Gilbert Stuart. Colonial Williamsburg Foundation, Williamsburg, Virginia

Alexis de Tocqueville, 1805–1859. The Granger Collection, New York

The Courtroom in the Supreme Court Building, Washington, D.C. Photo: Lee Troell Anderson

paper or see a particular movie, even when they decide not to become involved in an issue and leave it to others to decide for them. These decisions are constitutional in nature, may have lingering effects that spread like ripples in a pond, and are often not subject to judicial review. Judge Learned Hand, in an address called "The Spirit of Liberty," emphasized the people's importance in a democracy when he said:

> I often wonder whether we do not rest our hopes too much upon constitutions, upon laws, and upon courts. These are false hopes; believe me these are false hopes. Liberty lies in the hearts of men and women; when it dies there, no constitution, no law, no court can save it; no constitution, no law, no court can even do much to help it. While it lies there it needs no constitution, no law, no court to save it.

Judge Learned Hand. July 21, 1949. UPI/Bettmann Newsphotos

The Constitution itself relies upon the wisdom of the people. It achieves the Framers' objective of energetic government—not through the establishment of efficient institutions, but by deliberately devising a limited system that relies on the creative dynamics of decision-making by consensus. The Constitution attempts to harness the political strength and vision of the people, because the people—more than is often acknowledged—have a role in construing what is, after all, *their* Constitution.

If this Bicentennial celebration accomplishes anything, it ought to be to call attention to the tasks assigned to the people by the Constitution. It is an opportunity to engage in the process George Mason of Virginia called a "frequent recurrence to fundamental principles." One of the strengths of the Constitution is its potential to reflect the character and values of the people it serves while, at the same time, restraining the zealous excesses that overwhelm them from time to time. Within those wide boundaries, the Constitution provides an opportunity to choose from a broad range of policy choices and confront the most vexing of political dilemmas. In this manner, each generation receives guidance from its predecessors, but with sufficient flexibility to judge anew the choices of the past. It acknowledges past successes, while it remains forward-looking. Thus, continuity is assured without weighing future generations down with choices at odds with intervening experiences. In addition, it allows the Constitution to speak to enduring principles unlikely to be obscured by frequent revision.

The Constitution, wrote Justice Felix Frankfurter, "is most significantly not a document but a stream of history." Throughout American history, the rights accorded to individuals have had to be reconciled with the rights of society, as defined by majority rule. The pervasive constitutional dilemma has been to balance the need for societal order with the protection of individual liberties. To accomplish its purposes, government was invested with broad powers by the Constitution and, at the same time, limited in the use of those powers against the individual. The points at which these concurrent, but opposing, threads of constitutional doctrine are balanced provide the arena for our social, political, and philosophical debates. It is this nexus that is too often left to others to explore—and sometimes to manipulate.

That is a state of affairs that can prove costly to all of us. As Justice Oliver Wendell Holmes, Jr., said of the law generally, the Constitution is "a magic mirror . . . reflect[ing] not only our own lives, but the lives of all men . . . disclosing every painful step and every world-shaking context by which mankind has worked and fought its way from savage isolation to organic social life." The basic generational choices that arise under the Constitution—too imposing to ignore—are the products of the popular will. They affect not only present generations, but generations yet to come. We have an obligation to posterity, as well as to ourselves, to strive for informed choices. Only an educated populace can fulfill that obligation under a Constitution that places the ultimate power of government in the hands of its citizens.

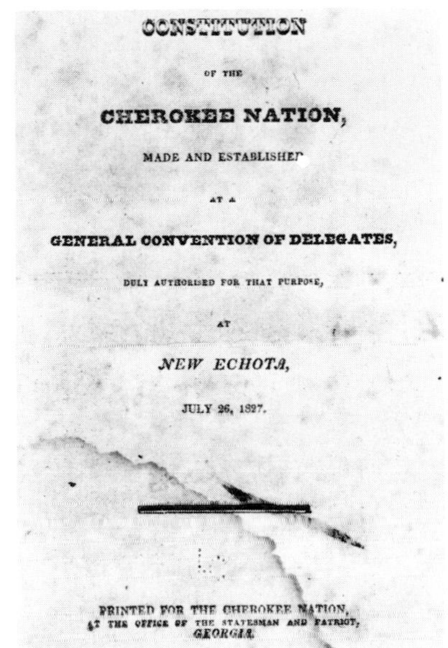

CONSTITUTION

OF THE

CHEROKEE NATION,

MADE AND ESTABLISHED

AT A

GENERAL CONVENTION OF DELEGATES,

DULY AUTHORISED FOR THAT PURPOSE,

AT

NEW ECHOTA,

JULY 26, 1827.

PRINTED FOR THE CHEROKEE NATION,
AT THE OFFICE OF THE STATESMAN AND PATRIOT,
GEORGIA.

Within the constitutional "stream of history," the Cherokees tried to retain their lands in 1827 by establishing a "nation" in northwestern Georgia and drafting a constitution based upon the United States Constitution. The Supreme Court declined to rule in a suit brought by the Cherokees against Georgia, holding that the Cherokees were not a foreign state. In *Cherokee Nation* v. *Georgia* (1831), Chief Justice John Marshall wrote: "This is not the tribunal which can redress the past or prevent the future." Constitution of the Cherokee Nation, New Echota, Georgia, 1827. Library of Congress, Washington, D.C.

Justice Oliver Wendell Holmes, Jr. on his eighty-fifth birthday. 1926. UPI/Bettmann Newsphotos

The changing of the guard in American judicial history, as reflected in this rendering of the Chief Justices of the United States, 1789–1888. Library of Congress, Washington, D.C.

On March 18, 1978, the first certified maximum containment laboratory for genetic research—a complex of sealed work boxes, sterilization equipment, and airlocks—was opened to public view in Frederick, Maryland. AP/Wide World Photos

Thus the Bicentennial is as much a challenge as an opportunity to celebrate. It is a challenge to us to work toward anticipating the bold frontiers that will open up in a world of computerized data systems, biotechnological advances, and other, yet unimagined developments that will place new power in the hands of society, while—at the same time—preserving the scheme of personal liberty the Constitution has come to symbolize.

Many of the decisions ahead will involve very difficult choices. Chief Justice Earl Warren cautioned that constitutional issues have "an iceberg quality containing beneath surface simplicity, submerged complexities which go to the very heart of a constitutional government." We will be called upon to make specific choices along the way, to reappraise those that have been made in the past, and to recognize that partisans will construct new conflicts from the vapors of the questions we leave unanswered.

The Constitution has succeeded as an experiment in self-government because it placed the most difficult tasks squarely upon the shoulders of the people. Let us celebrate this notable anniversary by equipping ourselves with the tools that will render us equal to the task.

Chief Justice Earl Warren on his seventy-fifth birthday. 1966. AP/Wide World Photos

Thomas Jefferson by Gilbert Stuart. 1805. Jointly owned by Monticello, the Thomas Jefferson Memorial Foundation, Incorporated, and the National Portrait Gallery, Smithsonian Institution. Purchase funds provided by the Regents of the Smithsonian Institution, the Trustees of the Thomas Jefferson Memorial Foundation, Incorporated, and the Enid and Crosby Kemper Foundation

PART I

Freedom of Conscience and Expression

If any liberty may be considered fundamental, it is the dual freedom of conscience and expression that is protected by the First Amendment. To the Framers, the term "conscience" referred to an individual's most personal beliefs, including those of a religious nature. They upheld the right of people to act on their beliefs, free from governmental interference, by permitting them to speak their minds and publish what they pleased. This is the very essence of the First Amendment. Still, the linkage of these abstract principles to real-life situations is often difficult to discern. Just as conscience and expression are joined in the Constitution, they have been joined as well in a running campaign that challenges the "wall of separation" Thomas Jefferson advocated as the proper constitutional approach to the relationship between Church and State.

In Hawkins County, Tennessee, Christian fundamentalists won one round in a legal dispute over the books used in the public school's reading program. Vicki Frost was arrested in 1983 for trespassing, after she tried to remove her second-grade daughter from a reading class. She had entered the classroom because she objected to the books being used in the class, calling them "anti-Christian." Subsequently, ten students were suspended for refusing to use the books. Among the books in dispute were *The Diary of Anne Frank*—objected to for being tolerant of all religions while fundamentalists believe there is only one true religion; and *The Wizard of Oz*—accused of promoting witchcraft and self-reliance, rather than trust in God. Frost and a group of other parents sued to require the schools to excuse their children from the reading program. They did not seek removal of the books from the schools. Federal district court judge Thomas Hull ruled in the parents' favor and ordered them reimbursed for private school expenses incurred while the issue was in dispute. School officials have appealed the order, but meanwhile have refused a group of students permission to stage *Anne Frank* as a play, on the ground that the fundamentalists might demand equal time. Even though Mrs. Frost was not trying to affect the rights of others, merely to assert her own rights, controversies such as these always have ripple effects.

In Mobile, Alabama, 624 Christian Evangelicals have sued the school board—with the support of a legal foundation affiliated with television evangelist Marion (Pat) Robertson—claiming that the public schools foist a religion called "secular humanism" on their children. They claim that this comprises an unconstitutional "establishment of religion" and want the curriculum and approximately forty-five textbooks changed. They define secular humanism as an anti-God, anti-American set of beliefs that puts man at the center of the universe, and they claim that it promotes sexual freedom, abortion, and other "immoral" practices. The plaintiffs in the lawsuit find support for their cause in a 1984 federal statute, lobbied through by fundamentalists, that prohibits the use of magnet-school funds for "any course of instruction the substance of which is secular humanism."

The Mobile plaintiffs range from those who object to textbooks and courses sanitized of all references to religion, to those who are refighting the battle over Darwinian evolution. That latter controversy does not seem to be one that will be easily laid to rest. In 1986, the Supreme Court heard a constitutional challenge to a 1981 Louisiana law that outlaws the teaching of evolution in the public schools unless "creation science" is also taught. Defenders of the law assert that it advances academic freedom by exposing students to scientific evidence supporting the Biblical story of creation and to what they describe as the scientific improbabilities of evolution. In addition, they say, it merely requires a balanced treatment of the two major theories concerning the origins of human beings. Opponents, however, claim that the law tries to pass off the Book of Genesis as science and enshrine a particular religious belief in the public schools.

The Wizard of Oz by L. Frank Baum. Cover illustration by Kathy Mitchell, © 1986 Kathy Mitchell. Used by permission of Western Publishing Co., Inc.

Charles Darwin. Copyrighted by the National Geographic Society. AP/ Wide World Photos

This fifteenth-century illustration of an episode from Genesis shows Adam and Eve in the Garden of Eden. "The Temptation and the Fall," fol. 25 from the Illuminated Manuscript *Les Très Riches Heures du Duc de Berry*. Musée Condé, Chantilly, France

The battle over textbooks is not confined to the so-called Bible Belt. More than 130 incidents were recorded in forty-four states in 1985. Many never reach the courtroom. For example, Susan Simonson, a parent of seven and a former public-school teacher, initiated a controversy in Corvallis, Oregon when she learned that her son's sex education class was a "how-to class instead of a not-to class." She later saw a film and read a pamphlet that warned of the dangers of secular humanism. Simonson organized a Committee for Quality School Textbooks, based upon her concern that the values being taught in the schools were at odds with her own. With 300 supporters, she attended an October 1982 school board meeting, demanding that books promoting secular humanism be taken out of the schools. An anti-censorship group took up the battle against Simonson's group, and the issue became the focus of the school board race in 1983, in which the people of the community decided that the dangers of censorship merited greater concern than the accusations Simonson had leveled at the school and its curricula.

The issues raised in these incidents call upon us to re-examine the way in which we view society's obligations. They also bring into focus the values at the core of the First Amendment: tolerance of other religious beliefs and tolerance of other political views. It is a difficult principle to uphold. Many of the first settlers in the New World fled their homelands to escape religious persecution, and an environment where Church and State were one. To criticize the state, under such a regime, was not only treason, but also heresy. Failing to support the official religion excluded one not just from the community of believers, but from all community affairs. In England, criticism of the King was a serious charge, whether it was in his capacity as ruler or as head of the Anglican Church. The Court of the Star Chamber punished religious dissenters relentlessly and, at the same time, was responsible for licensing and censoring publications. Even after the passage of the English Bill of Rights in 1689, and the expiration of licensing laws in 1695, there was little tolerance of religious or political dissent. A satiric attack upon the Church of England for punishing dissenting clergy landed *Robinson Crusoe* author Daniel Defoe in prison in 1702.

Freedom of religion and freedom of speech were simply opposite sides of the same coin. To uphold one required that the other be upheld as well. If freedom was to be realized, there could be no governmentally imposed orthodoxy, whether in religion or in politics. Furthermore, the two needed to be kept separate. Religious freedom required that government not meddle in church affairs, but equally important was the necessity to distance church officials from the reins of gov-

An early Plymouth Meeting House, built in 1683 and taken down in 1744. Pilgrim Society, Plymouth, Massachusetts

Daniel Defoe. Culver Pictures

An early printing press. Library of Congress, Washington, D.C.

ernment, so that the rights of religious dissenters would be protected.

While those who sought religious and political freedom by coming to the New World spoke in grandiloquent terms of their love of liberty, there were definite limits to their tolerance of others. In 1637, Anne Hutchinson was exiled from the Massachusetts Bay Colony for—together with other heresies—preaching that God's will is not just expressed in the Bible. The leaders of Massachusetts felt her views were a danger to the ordered way of life that had been established there.

The notion of the greater good has always been the justification for violations of individual rights. It is an appealing rationale. The difficulty lies in trying to define that greater good in an impartial manner. Those in power will tend to define it in terms of their self-interest, identifying their personal well-being with the stability and proper functioning of the state. An important colonial trial placed one version of this issue before a jury. John Peter Zenger was a skilled printer who agreed to publish the *New-York Weekly Journal* for a group of the colony's leading lawyers. The newspaper's first issue appeared on November 5, 1733 and immediately attracted a popular following for its witty attacks on the corrupt and incompetent Governor William Cosby, as well as for its paeans to liberty. Cosby was incensed and viewed the newspaper articles as attacks on the King's own authority. Cosby's supporters in the General Assembly pushed through a resolution ordering that copies of the offending newspaper be burned in a public square by the sheriff's "own Negroe."

Zenger was subsequently jailed "for printing and publishing several Seditious Libels." His original attorneys, James Alexander and William Smith—the anonymous authors of a number of the offending articles—were disbarred for conducting too zealous a pre-trial defense. The beginning of Zenger's trial on August 4, 1735 attracted an overflow audience. The drama was heightened when Andrew Hamilton, the most able and famous lawyer in the colonies, emerged from among the spectators to undertake Zenger's defense. (Hamilton had been secretly hired by Zenger's former attorneys, arriving in town from his home in Philadelphia just in time for the trial.)

Hamilton used an innovative defense against the charges. He admitted that his client had published the articles in question, but argued that the words had to be false for the jury to convict. At the time, libel was proven simply by demonstrating that scandalous material had been published, whether truthful or not. Hamilton asked the jury to decide both the rule of law to be applied, as well as to fulfill its traditional role as judge of the facts in the case.

View of Broad Street, Wall Street, and Federal Hall. 1797. Site of Peter Zenger's trial in 1735. I.N. Phelps Stokes Collection, Miriam and Ira D. Wallach Division of Art, Prints and Photographs, The New York Public Library, Astor, Lenox and Tilden Foundations

Roger Sherman by Ralph Earl. 1775. Yale University Art Gallery, New Haven. Gift of Roger Sherman White

The jury acquitted Zenger, upholding the right to tell the truth about those in power, even if it put the government into disrepute. The case had no precedential value, but was of enormous symbolic significance. Gouverneur Morris, who was responsible for much of the Constitution's eloquent language, said, "The trial of Zenger in 1735 was the morningstar of that liberty which subsequently revolutionized America."

By the time the Constitutional Convention met in Philadelphia, the freedoms of religion and speech had become well-accepted principles, even if not entirely accepted practices. Still, guarantees of those freedoms were not original parts of the Constitution. At the Convention, Charles Pinckney of South Carolina proposed that "[t]he liberty of the Press shall be inviolably preserved" and that "[n]o religious test or qualification shall ever be annexed to any oath of office under the authority of the U.S." Though the second of these proposals was adopted, Roger Sherman of Connecticut convinced delegates that the other provision was "unnecessary—The power of Congress does not extend to the Press." As Justice Joseph Story later explained, the no-religious-test provision was intended "to cut off forever, every pretence of any alliance between Church and State in national government."

The Antifederalists campaigned against ratification of the Constitution, in part, because it had no bill of rights. The Constitution's supporters not only viewed an enumeration of rights as unnecessary, but also thought that the danger of an incomplete listing mitigated against the attempt. They were sure that some individuals would point to any omissions and claim that the Framers never intended to give people something that, upon further reflection, might be considered a great natural right of mankind. Ironically, while the Bill of Rights is regarded as one of the Constitution's most appealing accomplishments, the fear that certain implicit rights would be disparaged has also been proven correct.

The Antifederalists succeeded in obtaining a promise that a bill of rights would be added to the 1787 Constitution. At the First Congress, meeting where Federal Hall now stands (and where the Zenger trial had taken place fifty-four years earlier), James Madison introduced fifteen amendments. Congress approved twelve for submission to the states, ten of which were ultimately ratified. First among them: "Congress shall make no law respecting an establishment of religion, or prohibiting the free exercise thereof; or abridging the freedom of speech, or of the press; or the right of the people peaceably to assemble, and to petition the Government for a redress of grievances."

The First Amendment established a system of freedom for

Patrick Henry, a fiery Antifederalist, is shown here addressing the Virginia Assembly. Historical Pictures Service, Chicago

Federal Hall, where the First Congress met in 1789. This is the only known contemporary view of George Washington's Inauguration as President of the United States of America. The Edward W. C. Arnold Collection, lent by The Metropolitan Museum of Art. Photograph courtesy Museum of The City of New York

Thomas Jefferson as seen through the eyes of his friend, Thaddeus Kosciuszko, a Polish patriot and American Revolutionary soldier. Courtesy, The Henry Francis du Pont Winterthur Museum

both belief and expression. The religious clauses owed a debt to Madison's successful fight earlier against an assessment in Virginia to support "Teachers of the Christian Religion," that had the powerful support of Patrick Henry. To persuade the legislature to defeat the bill, Madison prepared a *Memorial and Remonstrance*: "The Religion then of every man must be left to the conviction and conscience of every man; and it is the right of every man to exercise it as these may dictate.... In some instances [ecclesiastical establishments] have been seen to erect a spiritual tyranny on the ruins of Civil authority; in many instances they have been seen upholding the thrones of political tyranny; in no instances have they been seen the guardians of the liberties of the people."

In place of the assessment, Madison secured passage on January 16, 1786 of one of Jefferson's proudest achievements, the Virginia Statute of Religious Liberty, realizing the goals that were later incorporated into the First Amendment. That Amendment's ban on "establishment of religion" applied only to Congress until "incorporated"—i.e., applied also to the states—through the due process provisions of the Fourteenth Amendment, guaranteeing the rights to life, liberty, and property. At the time the First Amendment was adopted, six states had official churches or established religions. Litigation and growing sentiment against official religions caused all to abandon this practice. Massachusetts was the last to join the fold in 1833 when voters (by a ten-to-one margin) passed an amendment to their state constitution, eliminating taxes on behalf of religion. It was only then that the goal of religious freedom for all could truly be considered an American achievement.

Freedom of speech had a similarly uncertain start. In 1798, the Federalists passed the Alien and Sedition Acts to harrass their Republican opposition. The Acts made it a crime to "write, print, utter or publish" material unfavorable to the government, seemingly reestablishing the law of seditious libel, although explicitly providing for truth as a defense. The Acts were extremely unpopular and provoked vehement discussion. None of the twenty-five arrests or fifteen indictments under the Acts made it to the Supreme Court, but lower courts upheld the Acts against constitutional challenge. Thomas Jefferson pardoned all those who had been convicted under the Acts, which expired the day before his presidency began. In a 1964 decision, Justice William J. Brennan, Jr. acknowledged that "the great controversy over the Sedition Act of 1798... first crystallized a national awareness of the central meaning of the First Amendment.... Although the Sedition Act was never tested in this Court, the attack upon its validity has carried the day in the court of history."

Study for a portrait of John Adams by John Singleton Copley. The Metropolitan Museum of Art, Harris Brisbane Dick Fund, 1960

FIFTH *CONGRESS* OF THE UNITED STATES:

At the Second Session,

Begun and held at the city of *Philadelphia*, in the ſtate of PENNSYLVANIA, on *Monday*, the thirteenth of *November*, one thouſand ſeven hundred and ninety-ſeven.

An ACT *in addition to the act, entitled "An Act for the punishment of certain crimes against the United States."*

BE it enacted by the Senate and House of Representatives of the United States of America, in Congress assembled, *That if any persons shall unlawfully combine or conspire together, with intent to oppose any measure or measures of the government of the United States, which are or shall be directed by proper authority, or to impede the operation of any law of the United States, or to intimidate or prevent any person, holding a place or office in or under the government of the United States, from undertaking, performing or executing his trust or duty; and if any person or persons, with intent as aforesaid, shall counsel, advise or attempt to procure any insurrection, riot, unlawful assembly, or combination, whether such conspiracy, threatening, counsel, advice, or attempt shall have the proposed effect or not, he or they shall be deemed guilty of a high misdemeanor, and on conviction, before any court of the United States having jurisdiction thereof, shall be punished by a fine not exceeding five thousand dollars, and by imprisonment during a term not less than six months nor exceeding five years; and further, at the discretion of the court may be holden to find sureties for his good behaviour in such sum, and for such time, as the said court may direct.*

Sect. 2. And be it further enacted, That if any person shall write, print, utter or publish, or shall cause or procure to be written, printed, uttered or published, or shall knowingly and willingly assist or aid in writing, printing, uttering or publishing any false, scandalous and malicious writing or writings against the government of the United States, or either House of the Congress of the United States, or the President of the United States, with intent to defame the said government, or either House of the said Congress, or the said President, or to bring them, or either of them, into contempt or disrepute; or to excite against them, or either or any of them, the hatred of the good people of the United States, or to stir up sedition within the United States, or to excite any unlawful combinations therein, for opposing or resisting any law of the United States, or any act of the President of the United States, done in pursuance of any such law, or of the powers in him vested by the Constitution of the United States, or to resist, oppose, or defeat any such law or act; or to aid, encourage or abet any hostile designs of any foreign nation against the United States, their people or government, then such person, being thereof convicted before any Court of the United States having jurisdiction thereof, shall be punished by a fine not exceeding two thousand dollars, and by imprisonment not exceeding two years.

Sect. 3. And be it further enacted and declared, That if any person shall be prosecuted under this act for the writing or publishing any libel aforesaid, it shall be lawful for the defendant, upon the trial of the cause, to give in evidence in his defence, the truth of the matter contained in the publication charged as a libel. And the jury who shall try the cause, shall have a right to determine the law and the fact, under the direction of the Court, as in other cases.

Sect. 4. And be it further enacted, That this act shall continue and be in force until the third day of March, one thousand eight hundred and one, and no longer: Provided, that the expiration of the act shall not prevent or defeat a prosecution and punishment of any offence against the law, during the time it shall be in force.

Jonathan Dayton Speaker of the House of Representatives.

Theodore Sedgwick President of the Senate, pro tempore.

Approved July 14 1798
John Adams
President of the United States

I certify that this Act did originate in the Senate.
Attest
Sam. A. Otis Secretary

The Sedition Act. 1798. National Archives, Washington, D.C.

A Class in the Old Lutheran Schoolhouse at York, Pennsylvania. Drawing by Lewis Miller. 1805. Historical Society of York County, PA.

The Alien and Sedition Acts recognized that the power to express opinions is always a threat to the stability of the existing hierarchy. In 1920, newspaperman Frank I. Cobb put it another way: "The Bill of Rights is a born rebel. It reeks with sedition. In every clause it shakes its fist in the face of constituted authority . . . it is the one guarantee of human freedom to the American people." Cobb was emphasizing the essence of the freedoms protected by the First Amendment, as well as the discomfort it is bound to cause.

Perhaps nowhere do those values cause greater discomfort than in the classrooms of the public school. There is a general expectation that our schools will teach children to respect authority, will impart vital social skills, and will provide an understanding of the American system of rights and responsibilities. At the same time, it is hoped that children will emerge from their educational experience with well-developed critical and analytical faculties so that they may be able to meet the demands of adult life and the duties of self-government. That means respect for authority and order must be tempered with tolerance for those who question that authority and sometimes disrupt the prevailing order. It is a difficult balance to achieve.

The advent of public education was bound to make classrooms a battleground over ideas. Almost from the start, a struggle began over the place of religion in the schools. Horace Mann was forced to address it in his 1848 report as Secretary of Education in Massachusetts: "[A]bstinence from religious oppression, this acknowledgement of the rights of others, this explicit recognition and avowal of the supreme and exclusive jurisdiction of Heaven, and this denial of the right of any earthly power to encroach upon that jurisdiction, is precisely what the Massachusetts school-system purports to do in theory and what it does actually in practice. Hence I infer that our system is not an irreligious one, but is in the strictest accordance with religion and its obligations."

It was not, however, in the context of education that the Supreme Court had its first opportunity to construe the meaning of the Constitution's guarantee of religious freedom. In *Reynolds* v. *United States* (1878), a Mormon was convicted of bigamy in the Utah territory. He challenged the conviction on the grounds that "it was the duty of male [Mormons], circumstances permitting, to practise polygamy" and that failure to practice polygamy would be punishable by "damnation in the life to come."

Chief Justice Morrison R. Waite delivered the Court's opinion, upholding the conviction and making a distinction between laws that prohibit an activity with religious significance and those that affect a religious belief. "Laws are made

Horace Mann. Culver Pictures

Chief Justice Morrison R. Waite. AP/Wide World Photos

Although child labor came to be perceived as a social evil by many after the turn of the century, it was widespread in nineteenth-century America. Justice Oliver Wendell Holmes, Jr. registered a notable dissent in *Hammer* v. *Dagenhart* (1918)—a five-to-four decision declaring that a 1916 law forbidding child labor was unconstitutional. Many years later, Justice Holmes's 1918 dissent was eventually adopted in *United States* v. *Darby Lumber Company* (1941), a decision that specifically reversed *Hammer* v. *Dagenhart*, and upheld a 1938 law banning child labor.

Breaker Boys in Pennsylvania. 1908–1912. National Archives, Washington, D.C.

Doffers or bobbin removers in Tennessee. 1908–1912. National Archives, Washington, D.C.

Sheet and Tin workers in Pittsburgh. 1908. Pennsylvania Historical and Museum Commission, Harrisburg

A worker at a Southern Cotton Mill. 1908–1912. National Archives, Washington, D.C.

for the government of actions," he wrote, "and while they cannot interfere with mere religious belief and opinions, they may with practices. Suppose one believed that human sacrifices were a necessary part of religious worship, would it be seriously contended that the civil government under which he lived could not interfere to prevent a sacrifice?" Waite's opinion also questioned how a government could exist if a criminal could "escape punishment because he religiously believed the law which he had broken ought never to have been made."

Chief Justice Waite put the Supreme Court firmly on record in support of Thomas Jefferson's description of the First Amendment religious clauses as "building a wall of separation between Church and State." "Coming as this does from an acknowledged leader of the advocates of the measure," the Chief Justice wrote, "it may be accepted almost as an authoritative declaration of the scope and effect of the amendment thus secured."

The *Reynolds* decision was not considered a threat to religious freedom, partially because polygamy was not widely practiced and the decision affected so few. The next First Amendment challenges that reached the Supreme Court involved freedom of speech. The turn of the century had come hard on the heels of a severe recession, growing labor unrest, and a war with Spain. The tenets of European social liberalism had excited those searching for new ideas with which to address the manifold problems facing America. But there were others who considered such ideas dangerous. By 1917, World War I loomed large in everyone's mind, and the United States passed an Espionage Act, strengthened through 1918 amendments, to support the war effort by punishing anyone who might aid the enemy, obstruct recruitment, or cause disloyalty. It even banned "disloyal, profane, scurrilous, or abusive language" directed against the government or the armed forces.

One of the first convictions under the Act was for circulating a document advocating that people "Assert Your Rights," and calling the war conscription effort a violation of the Thirteenth Amendment's ban on slavery. The defendants were charged with causing insubordination in the armed services and obstructing recruitment and enlistment. The case gave the Supreme Court an opportunity to explore the limits of free speech.

"The most stringent protection of free speech would not protect a man in falsely shouting fire in a theatre and causing a panic. . . . " wrote Justice Oliver Wendell Holmes, Jr., for a unanimous Court in *Schenck* v. *United States* (1919). "The question in every case is whether the words used are used in such circumstances and are of such a nature as to create a clear and

Justice Oliver Wendell Holmes, Jr. and Justice Louis D. Brandeis. Collection of the Supreme Court of the United States, Washington, D.C.

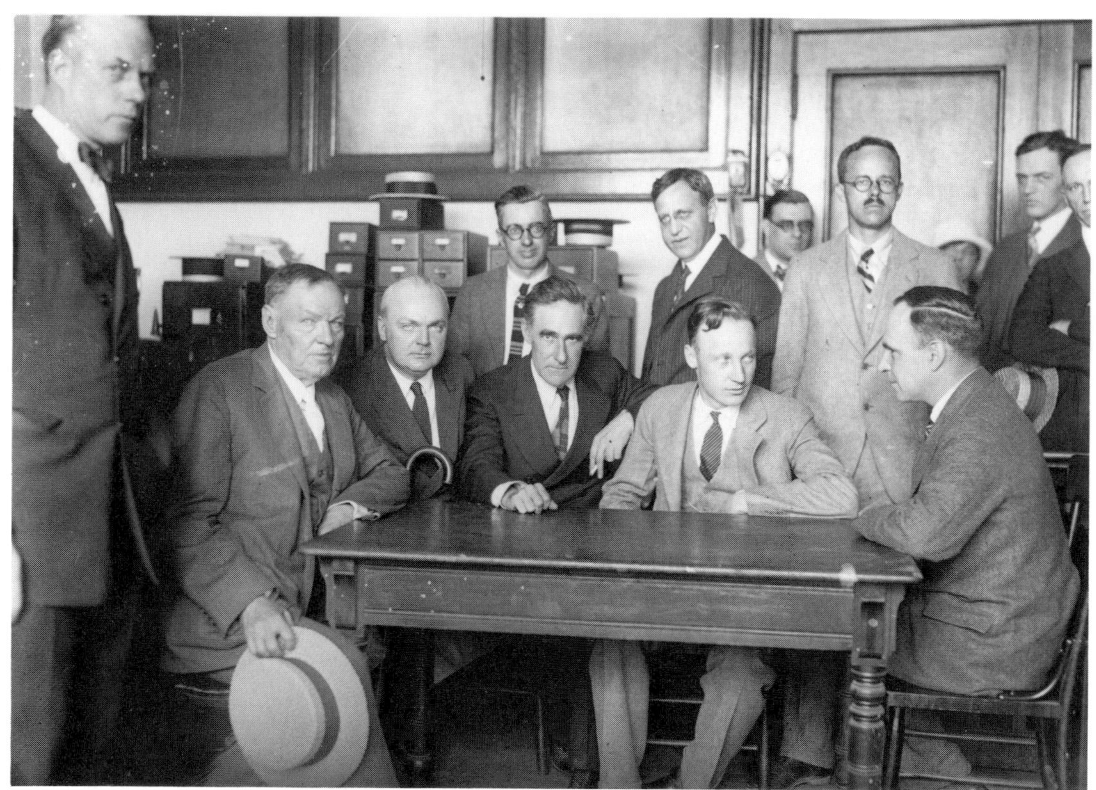

Participants in the Scopes trial. 1925. Seated here are Clarence Darrow, D.F. Malone, Dr. J.R. Neal, and John T. Scopes. UPI/Bettmann Newsphotos

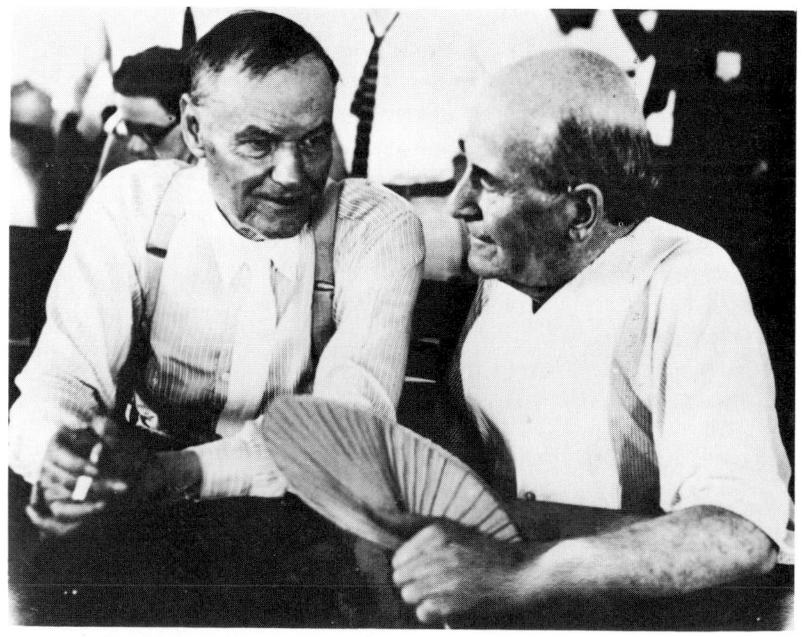

Clarence Darrow and William Jennings Bryan at the Scopes trial. 1925.
Chicago Historical Society

present danger that they will bring about the substantive evils that Congress has a right to prevent. . . . When a nation is at war many things that might be said in time of peace are such a hindrance to its effort that their utterance will not be endured so long as men fight . . . "

Schenck was the first of a series of cases through which First Amendment doctrine took shape. By 1925, the Supreme Court had decided that the Fourteenth Amendment made the Constitution's free expression guarantee applicable against state regulation, even when the regulation affected education. In *Meyer* v. *Nebraska* (1923), the Court declared a state statute that prohibited teaching in a language other than English unconstitutional as a violation of due process and academic freedom. The Court also struck down a state law that set up a public-school monopoly by denying parents and students the freedom to choose private or parochial schools in *Pierce* v. *Society of Sisters* (1925). The two cases upheld the central importance of expressive and religious freedom, respectively.

The year 1925 also saw the nation's attention drawn to Dayton, Tennessee where a battle took place that has many parallels to today's important concerns over the freedoms of conscience and expression. On March 21, 1925, the fundamentalist-dominated Tennessee legislature made it a crime for anyone in a publicly supported educational institution "to teach any theory that denies the story of the Divine Creation of man as taught in the Bible, and to teach instead that man has descended from a lower order of animals."

A plan was hatched to test the law's constitutionality. John T. Scopes, a twenty-four-year-old substitute biology teacher, volunteered to be the defendant. Supporting Scopes was a group of local businessmen interested in putting Dayton on the map; when Scopes was arrested, they immediately alerted the press: "We've just arrested a man for teaching evolution."

William Jennings Bryan, a former Secretary of State and three-time Democratic presidential candidate, volunteered to direct the prosecution. He had drafted an anti-evolution statute for Florida and predicted more states would follow. Clarence Darrow, the most celebrated criminal defense lawyer of the day, represented Scopes. More than one hundred journalists descended on Dayton, including H. L. Mencken who caustically described the locals as "yokels." A circus atmosphere pervaded the town, with signs urging "Read Your Bible" and "God is Love." Called the "monkey trial," the case inspired vendors to sell items with that theme, including pins that read "Your Old Man's a Monkey."

Bryan transformed the trial into a struggle between God and evil. "The contest between evolution and Christianity is a

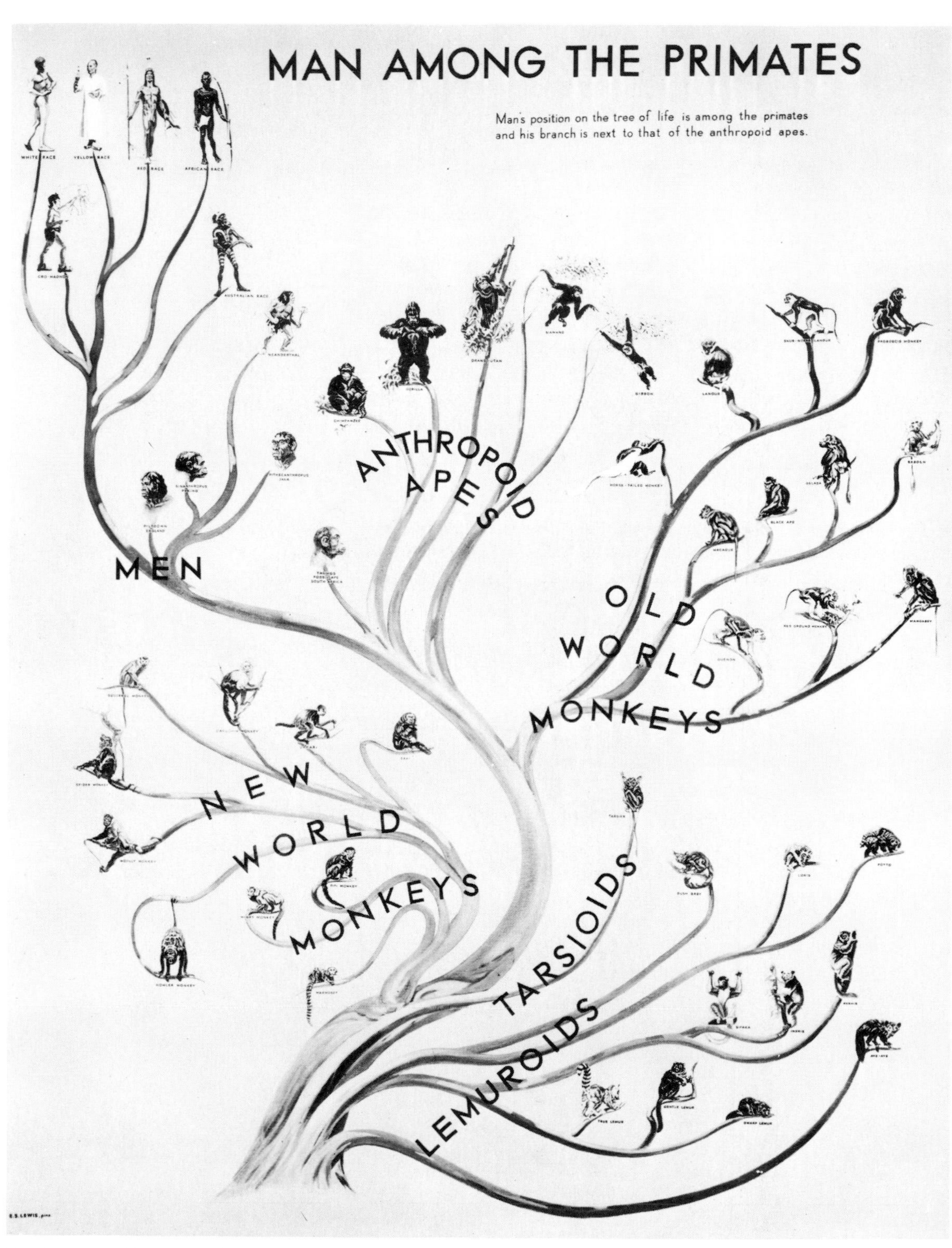
MAN AMONG THE PRIMATES
Man's position on the tree of life is among the primates and his branch is next to that of the anthropoid apes.
MEN
ANTHROPOID APES
OLD WORLD MONKEYS
NEW WORLD MONKEYS
TARSIOIDS
LEMUROIDS

Evolutionary Chart. Neg./Trans. No. 315595. (Photo by Irving Dutcher and H.S. Rice). Courtesy Department Library Services, American Museum of Natural History, New York

The jury in the courtroom at the Scopes trial. 1925. Library of Congress, Washington, D.C.

duel to the death," he told a crowd that greeted him at the train station. "If evolution wins in Dayton, Christianity goes—not suddenly, of course, but gradually—for the two cannot stand together."

The eleven day trial opened on July 10, 1925 with a prayer, Darrow's objection being overruled, and with jurors "unanimously hot for Genesis," according to Mencken. Darrow's most spectacular tactic during the trial was to call Bryan himself as an expert witness on the Bible and make him look foolish in a ridiculously literal interpretation.

"If today you can take a thing like evolution and make it a crime to teach it in the public school," Darrow argued in summation, "tomorrow you can make it a crime to teach it in the private schools, and the next year you can make it a crime to teach it on the hustings or in the church. At the next session you may ban books and newspapers. Soon you may set Catholic against Protestant and Protestant against Protestant, and try to foist your own religion upon the minds of men. If you can do one you can do the other."

Of the speech, Mencken noted: "It rose like a wind and ended like a flourish of bugles. . . . But the morons in the audience, when it was over, simply hissed it." The jury found Scopes guilty, but the newspaper accounts helped discredit the verdict. Upon sentencing, Scopes told the judge, "I will continue in the future, as I have in the past, to oppose this law in any way I can. Any other action would be in violation of my ideal of academic freedom—that is, to teach the truth as guaranteed in our Constitution, of personal and religious freedom."

Justice Abe Fortas. 1968. UPI/ Bettmann Newsphotos

Scopes was fined $100, but the Tennessee supreme court unanimously reversed the fine—although they left the conviction itself standing—because the judge, rather than the jury, had set the sum. Tennessee did not repeal that anti-evolution law until April 1967, although it was not enforced in the interim. In *Epperson* v. *Arkansas* (1968), a similarly-worded statute dating back to 1928 was found unconstitutional by the Supreme Court. Justice Abe Fortas wrote that the Arkansas law "selects from the body of knowledge a particular segment which it proscribes for the sole reason that it is deemed to conflict with a particular religious doctrine." The state cannot, he added, "promote one religion or religious theory against another or even against the militant opposite."

The difficulty the Court has faced in upholding religious freedom in the school setting was evident in the flag-salute cases. A Pennsylvania statute required schoolchildren to salute the American flag and recite the Pledge of Allegiance. Two children, Jehovah's Witnesses, were expelled after they refused to participate because they believed it violated the Bible's command against worshiping graven images. In *Minersville District* v. *Gobitis* (1940), the Court found that the interest in national unity exemplified by the flag-salute ceremony had to prevail over the children's religious convictions. The Court then reconsidered the issue in *West Virginia State Board of Education* v. *Barnette* (1943), and overruled their earlier decision. Again, the children expelled were Jehovah's Witnesses who objected, on religious grounds, to a compulsory flag salute.

This time, the Court viewed the case not as a challenge to national unity, but as a governmental intrusion into freedom of belief and expression. Justice Robert H. Jackson wrote for the majority that "the action of the local authorities in compelling the flag salute and pledge transcends constitutional limitations on their power and invades the sphere of intellect and spirit which it is the purpose of the First Amendment to our Constitution to reserve from all official control."

Similar considerations were raised in *Wisconsin* v. *Yoder* (1972). Jonas Yoder and several other members of an Amish community were convicted of violating the state's compulsory school-attendance laws by removing their children from school after completing the eighth grade. The defendants were fined five dollars each for taking their children out of school before the age of sixteen. Yoder objected to continued schooling because, according to Chief Justice Warren Burger's opinion, "Amish society emphasizes informal learning-through-doing, a life of 'goodness,' rather than a life of intellect, wisdom, rather than technical knowledge, community welfare rather than competition, and separation, rather than integration with con-

First and second graders reciting the Pledge of Allegiance at an Elementary School in Massachusetts. 1985. AP/Wide World Photos

Justice Robert H. Jackson. 1942. AP/Wide World Photos

Two Amish boys and a horse-drawn plow in a Pennsylvania field. 1979. UPI/Bettmann Newsphotos

Justice Hugo Black. 1952. UPI/ Bettmann Newsphotos

temporary worldly society." The deeply held religious convictions of the Amish prevailed over the state's interest in assuring an educated populace. The Court found no particular benefit in this case from another few years of formal education, while noting that the agricultural way of life of the Amish was served by the informal learning that would continue in the Amish community.

While these decisions demonstrate that the First Amendment limits the scope of governmental interference with private religious practices, the courts have had the most difficulty in grappling with the types of governmental assistance the Constitution permits to religious schools. The issue first reached the Supreme Court in *Everson* v. *Board of Education* (1947). A New Jersey board of education permitted parents of private and parochial schoolchildren to be reimbursed for using public transportation to get their children to school. The only private school in the district was a Catholic school, and the program worked only to the benefit of students attending that school. Nevertheless, by a five-to-four vote, the Court upheld the program because it merely amounted to free bus service for all schoolchildren, public and private, and did not benefit religion directly.

Justice Hugo L. Black's opinion examined the constitutional principles involved in the case:

> The "establishment of religion" clause of the First Amendment, means at least this: Neither a state nor the Federal Government can set up a church. Neither can pass laws which aid one religion, aid all religions, or prefer one religion over another. Neither can force nor influence a person to go to or to remain away from church against his will or force him to profess a belief or disbelief in any religion. No person can be punished for entertaining or professing religious beliefs or disbeliefs, for church attendance or non-attendance. No tax in any amount, large or small, can be levied to support any religious activities or institutions, whatever they may be called, or whatever form they may adopt to teach or practice religion. Neither a state nor the Federal Government can, openly or secretly, participate in the affairs of any religious organizations or groups and vice versa.

Invoking Thomas Jefferson, Justice Black added, "The First Amendment has erected a wall between church and state. That wall must be kept high and impregnable. We could not approve the slightest breach." True to those words, in *McCollum* v. *Board of Education* (1948), the Court struck down a Champaign, Illinois "released time" program of religious instruction on public school grounds for children whose parents had signed request cards. Still, Jefferson's famous wall of sep-

Chief Justice Warren E. Burger. 1984. AP/Wide World Photos

aration has not been entirely impregnable. In *Zorach* v. *Clauson* (1952), the Court found no constitutional impediment to a New York City released-time program that took place in church buildings and did not involve the expenditure of public funds.

In addition, the Court has approved tax exemptions for religious organizations, tuition tax credits for parents of parochial schoolchildren, Sunday closing laws, legislative chaplains and prayers, a governmentally sponsored Christmas display that includes a Nativity crèche, a textbook-loan program to parochial-school students, and certain types of financial assistance to religious schools, their students or parents.

Chief Justice Burger admitted in a 1971 decision that the Supreme Court "can only dimly perceive the lines of demarcation in this extraordinarily sensitive area of constitutional law." Still, he is the author of the three-part test the courts presently use to determine whether governmental assistance to religion violates the First Amendment's establishment clause. Under this test, a program fails to pass constitutional muster if: (1) it does not have a secular purpose, (2) it has a primary effect of advancing or inhibiting religion, *or* (3) it causes an excessive entanglement between government and religion. In *Lemon* v. *Kurtzman* (1971), a Rhode Island law that provided salary supplements to parochial-school teachers who teach secular subjects in order to maintain equality of educa-

Children praying in a Pennsylvania Elementary School. 1984. AP/Wide World Photos

tion with the public schools failed the test, in part, because governmental monitoring to assure that no religious purpose was being served would necessarily involve excessive entanglement.

No religious issue, though, has been as controversial as the one involving prayer in the public schools. The issue reached the Supreme Court in 1962 over a required recitation of a non-denominational prayer composed by the New York Board of Regents: "Almighty God, we acknowledge our dependence upon Thee, and we beg Thy blessings upon us, our parents, our teachers and our country." The Court's decision holding the prayer and recitation in public schools unconstitutional brought more protest mail than any other case the Court had ever decided.

"When the power, prestige and financial support of government is placed behind a particular religious belief," wrote Justice Hugo L. Black, "the indirect coercive pressure upon religious minorities to conform to the prevailing officially approved religion is plain." He warned that school-mandated prayer established "a union of government and religion [that] tends to destroy government and to degrade religion."

The issue returned to the Court the following year in two related cases: one brought by Unitarians in Abington Township, Pennsylvania over public-school Bible readings and another brought by atheists in Baltimore over opening the school day with the Lord's Prayer. In holding that both practices violate the establishment clause, Justice Tom Clark's opinion relied on the fact that the religious activities were "held in school buildings under the supervision and with the participation of teachers employed in those schools."

Ever since these school-prayer decisions, proposals for constitutional amendments to overturn the Court's decisions have been a constant in constitutional debate. But politicians who have addressed the issue are wrong when they claim that the Court "took God out of the classroom." The decision merely prohibited officially sponsored religious exercises. The danger the Court recognized is that religious freedom is impaired by governmental endorsement of a particular way of praying. Still, as a *New York Times* columnist put it, as long as there are math tests, there will always be prayer in schools. The school-prayer decisions also do not bar schools from teaching comparative religion, the history of religion, or religious influences in fields such as philosophy or ethics.

In two more recent cases, the Court reaffirmed its approach to these issues. In *Stone* v. *Graham* (1980), it held a Kentucky law requiring the posting of the Ten Commandments unconstitutional, because the purpose of the law was "plainly religious in nature." In *Wallace* v. *Jaffree* (1985), the Court found the constitutional prohibition against establishing religion violated by an Alabama law that required the school day to begin with a moment of silence for "meditation or voluntary prayer." In a concurring opinion, Justice Sandra Day O'Connor wrote: "[T]he crucial question is whether the State has conveyed or attempted to convey the message that children should use the moment of silence for prayer." She and the majority concluded that the Alabama law "endorses the decision to pray" and "sponsors a religious exercise."

While the government cannot sponsor prayer, it also cannot interfere with the prayers that are spoken in houses of worship. That is the dual message of the First Amendment's religious clauses. Another arena where words cannot be affected by government wishes is in the press. The issue of whether speech can be suppressed in advance—prior restraint—was first addressed in a case that involved a particularly sleazy newspaper. A Minnesota statute empowered its courts to enjoin as a nuisance any "malicious, scandalous and defamatory newspaper, magazine or other periodical." *The Saturday Press* fit that description perfectly. Jay M. Near, its publisher, was hopelessly bigoted and proud of it. His newspaper was permanently shut down by law, after it began running a series charging the chief of police with corruption and the Minneapolis mayor and county attorney with dereliction of duty.

Justice Tom C. Clark with his son, W. Ramsey Clark, when the latter was admitted to practice before the Supreme Court. UPI/Bettmann Newsphotos

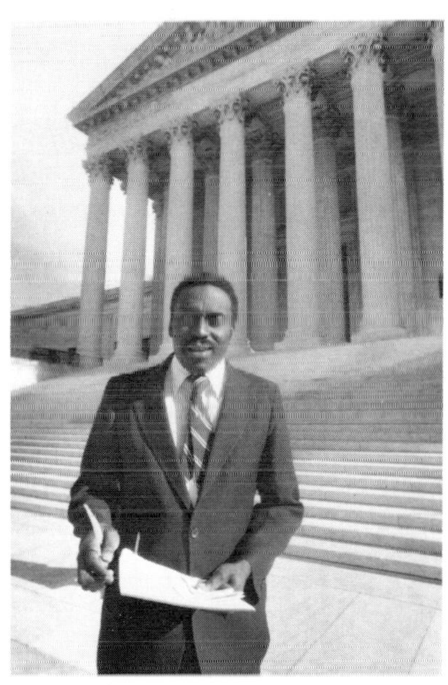

Ishmael Jaffree of Mobile, Alabama, standing outside the Supreme Court where his case challenging a moment of silent prayer in schools was being heard. 1984. UPI/Bettmann Newsphotos

The new Supreme Court Chamber in the Capitol, 1861–1935 (now the restored old Senate Chamber). Office of the Architect of the Capitol, Washington, D.C.

"The fact that the liberty of the press may be abused by miscreant purveyors of scandal," wrote Chief Justice Charles Evans Hughes, "does not make any the less necessary the immunity of the press from previous restraint in dealing with official misconduct." The decision in *Near* v. *Minnesota* (1931) recognizing "the primary need of a vigilant and courageous press" was a dramatic victory for free press principles, although it left open the question as to whether *any* circumstances might allow prior censorship of the news. It also suggested that the remedy for those who felt slandered was through libel actions.

Libel laws are designed to prevent the publication of false information damaging to the reputation of an individual. When that person is a public official, however, a First Amendment issue arises because a lawsuit alleging libel can become a weapon to deter criticism of official conduct—the right to engage in such criticism being one of the main purposes in guaranteeing a free press. The Supreme Court addressed the issue after a group of civil rights activists took a full-page advertisement in the March 29, 1960 issue of *The New York Times* under the title, "Heed Their Rising Voices." The advertisement contended that "an unprecedented wave of terror" had been directed against the activists' peaceful attempts to uphold their constitutional rights. The advertisement charged police in Montgomery, Alabama with terrorizing student protesters, and accused "Southern violators" of bombing the home of Dr. Mar-

Advertisement

THE NEW YORK TIMES, TUESDAY, MARCH 29, 1960. L 25

"*The growing movement of peaceful mass demonstrations by Negroes is something new in the South, something understandable. . . . Let Congress heed their rising voices, for they will be heard.*"

—*New York Times editorial Saturday, March 19, 1960*

Heed Their Rising Voices

As the whole world knows by now, thousands of Southern Negro students are engaged in wide-spread non-violent demonstrations in positive affirmation of the right to live in human dignity as guaranteed by the U. S. Constitution and the Bill of Rights. In their efforts to uphold these guarantees, they are being met by an unprecedented wave of terror by those who would deny and negate that document which the whole world looks upon as setting the pattern for modern freedom. . . .

In Orangeburg, South Carolina, when 400 students peacefully sought to buy doughnuts and coffee at lunch counters in the business district, they were forcibly ejected, tear-gassed, soaked to the skin in freezing weather with fire hoses, arrested en masse and herded into an open barbed-wire stockade to stand for hours in the bitter cold.

In Montgomery, Alabama, after students sang "My Country, 'Tis of Thee" on the State Capitol steps, their leaders were expelled from school, and truck-loads of police armed with shotguns and tear-gas ringed the Alabama State College Campus. When the entire student body protested to state authorities by refusing to re-register, their dining hall was pad-locked in an attempt to starve them into submission.

In Tallahassee, Atlanta, Nashville, Savannah, Greensboro, Memphis, Richmond, Charlotte, and a host of other cities in the South, young American teen-agers, in face of the entire weight of official state apparatus and police power, have boldly stepped forth as protagonists of democracy. Their courage and amazing restraint have inspired millions and given a new dignity to the cause of freedom.

Small wonder that the Southern violators of the Constitution fear this new, non-violent brand of freedom fighter . . . even as they fear the upswelling right-to-vote movement. Small wonder that they are determined to destroy the one man who, more than any other, symbolizes the new spirit now sweeping the South—the Rev. Dr. Martin Luther King, Jr., world-famous leader of the Montgomery Bus Protest. For it is his doctrine of non-violence which has inspired and guided the students in their widening wave of sit-ins; and it this same Dr. King who founded and is president of the Southern Christian Leadership Conference—the organization which is spearheading the surging right-to-vote movement. Under Dr. King's direction the Leadership Conference conducts Student Workshops and Seminars in the philosophy and technique of non-violent resistance.

Again and again the Southern violators have answered Dr. King's peaceful protests with intimidation and violence. They have bombed his home almost killing his wife and child. They have assaulted his person. They have arrested him seven times—for "speeding," "loitering" and similar "offenses." And now they have charged him with "perjury"—a *felony* under which they could imprison him for *ten years*. Obviously, their real purpose is to remove him physically as the leader to whom the students and millions of others—look for guidance and support, and thereby to intimidate *all* leaders who may rise in the South. Their strategy is to behead this affirmative movement, and thus to demoralize Negro Americans and weaken their will to struggle. The defense of Martin Luther King, spiritual leader of the student sit-in movement, clearly, therefore, is an integral part of the total struggle for freedom in the South.

Decent-minded Americans cannot help but applaud the creative daring of the students and the quiet heroism of Dr. King. But this is one of those moments in the stormy history of Freedom when men and women of good will must do more than applaud the rising-to-glory of others. The America whose good name hangs in the balance before a watchful world, the America whose heritage of Liberty these Southern Upholders of the Constitution are defending, is *our* America as well as theirs . . .

We must heed their rising voices—yes—but we must add our own.

We must extend ourselves above and beyond moral support and render the material help so urgently needed by those who are taking the risks, facing jail, and even death in a glorious re-affirmation of our Constitution and its Bill of Rights.

We urge you to join hands with our fellow Americans in the South by supporting, with your dollars, this Combined Appeal for all three needs—the defense of Martin Luther King—the support of the embattled students—and the struggle for the right-to-vote.

Your Help Is Urgently Needed . . . NOW !!

Stella Adler
Raymond Pace Alexander
Harry Van Arsdale
Harry Belafonte
Julie Belafonte
Dr. Algernon Black
Marc Blitztein
William Branch
Marlon Brando
Mrs. Ralph Bunche
Diahann Carroll
Dr. Alan Knight Chalmers
Richard Coe
Nat King Cole
Cheryl Crawford
Dorothy Dandridge
Ossie Davis
Sammy Davis, Jr.
Ruby Dee
Dr. Philip Elliott
Dr. Harry Emerson Fosdick
Anthony Franciosa
Lorraine Hansbury
Rev. Donald Harrington
Nat Hentoff
James Hicks
Mary Hinkson
Van Heflin
Langston Hughes
Morris Iushewitz
Mahalia Jackson
Mordecai Johnson
John Killens
Eartha Kitt
Rabbi Edward Klein
Hope Lange
John Lewis
Viveca Lindfors
Carl Murphy
Don Murray
John Murray
A. J. Muste
Frederick O'Neal
L. Joseph Overton
Clarence Pickett
Shad Polier
Sidney Poitier
A. Philip Randolph
John Raitt
Elmer Rice
Jackie Robinson
Mrs. Eleanor Roosevelt
Bayard Rustin
Robert Ryan
Maureen Stapleton
Frank Silvera
Hope Stevens
George Tabori
Rev. Gardner C. Taylor
Norman Thomas
Kenneth Tynan
Charles White
Shelley Winters
Max Youngstein

We in the south who are struggling daily for dignity and freedom warmly endorse this appeal

Rev. Ralph D. Abernathy (*Montgomery, Ala.*)
Rev. Fred L. Shuttlesworth (*Birmingham, Ala.*)
Rev. Kelley Miller Smith (*Nashville, Tenn.*)
Rev. W. A. Dennis (*Chattanooga, Tenn.*)
Rev. C. K. Steele (*Tallahassee, Fla.*)
Rev. Matthew D. McCollom (*Orangeburg, S. C.*)
Rev. William Holmes Borders (*Atlanta, Ga.*)
Rev. Douglas Moore (*Durham, N. C.*)
Rev. Wyatt Tee Walker (*Petersburg, Va.*)
Rev. Walter L. Hamilton (*Norfolk, Va.*)
I. S. Levy (*Columbia, S. C.*)
Rev. Martin Luther King, Sr. (*Atlanta, Ga.*)
Rev. Henry C. Bunton (*Memphis, Tenn.*)
Rev. S. S. Seay, Sr. (*Montgomery, Ala.*)
Rev. Samuel W. Williams (*Atlanta, Ga.*)
Rev. A. L. Davis (*New Orleans, La.*)
Mrs. Katie E. Whickham (*New Orleans, La.*)
Rev. W. H. Hall (*Hattiesburg, Miss.*)
Rev. J. E. Lowery (*Mobile, Ala.*)
Rev. T. J. Jemison (*Baton Rouge, La.*)

COMMITTEE TO DEFEND MARTIN LUTHER KING AND THE STRUGGLE FOR FREEDOM IN THE SOUTH

312 West 125th Street, New York 27, N. Y. UNiversity 6-1700

Chairmen: A. Philip Randolph, Dr. Gardner C. Taylor; *Chairmen of Cultural Division:* Harry Belafonte, Sidney Poitier; *Treasurer:* Nat King Cole; *Executive Director:* Bayard Rustin; *Chairmen of Church Division:* Father George B. Ford, Rev. Harry Emerson Fosdick, Rev. Thomas Kilgore, Jr., Rabbi Edward E. Klein; *Chairman of Labor Division:* Morris Iushewitz

Please mail this coupon TODAY!

Committee To Defend Martin Luther King
and
The Struggle For Freedom In The South
312 West 125th Street, New York 27, N. Y.
UNiversity 6-1700

I am enclosing my contribution of $______ for the work of the Committee.

Name ______ (PLEASE PRINT)
Address ______
City ______ Zone ___ State ______

☐ I want to help ☐ Please send further information

Please make checks payable to:

Committee To *Defend Martin Luther King*

"Heed Their Rising Voices" advertisement in the March 29, 1960 issue of *The New York Times*. Courtesy *The New York Times*

Justice William J. Brennan, Jr. 1976.
UPI/Bettmann Newsphotos

tin Luther King, Jr., assaulting him, and arresting him seven times. The charges were not entirely accurate—King had been arrested only four times, for example, as a check of the *Times* newspaper files could have shown. The advertisement concluded with a fund-raising appeal to support voting rights and Dr. King's legal defense.

L. B. Sullivan, a Montgomery commissioner whose supervisory responsibilities included the police, sued the activists and the *Times*, claiming that the advertisement libeled him in its derogatory references to the police. In holding that no libel had occurred, Justice William J. Brennan, Jr. observed that the Constitution provides "a profound national commitment to the principle that debate on public issues should be uninhibited, robust, and wide-open, and that it may well include vehement, caustic, and sometimes unpleasantly sharp attacks on government and public officials." The advertisement was found to be "an expression of grievance and protest on one of the major public issues of our time" and due constitutional protection.

The rationale behind this approach was explained by Justice Black: "I doubt that a country can live in freedom where its people can be made to suffer physically or financially for criticizing their government, its actions or its officials."

Based upon the standard established in *New York Times Co.* v. *Sullivan* (1964), a public official—later cases expanded this category to include public figures and matters of public concern—must prove a publication is false, defamatory, and published with reckless disregard of the truth, or actual malice, to constitute a libel.

Considerations of national security may also be insufficient to prevent publication of criticism directed against the government or public officials. In 1971, the antiwar movement was at its height, with student protesters challenging the very fabric of society. Students had been killed during demonstrations at Kent State and Jackson State Universities, and an anxious Nixon administration was engaged in illegal domestic spying activities that were to culminate in the Watergate scandal. That administration, already feeling itself under attack, acted swiftly in seeking injunctions when it learned that *The New York Times* and *The Washington Post* were about to publish a series of documents that came to be known as the "Pentagon Papers."

These Papers were a classified, multi-volume study of United States involvement in Vietnam obtained by the newspapers from Daniel Ellsberg, a former government employee who had become strongly opposed to the American war effort. The documents contained no technical data on weapons, or information concerning still-valid intelligence information that could have jeopardized existing United States interests in Vietnam. The injunctions, sought under the claim of national security, were primarily aimed at preventing the information from fueling domestic opposition to the war.

The case reached the Supreme Court as *New York Times* v. *United States* (1971) on an expedited basis, just seventeen days after it was filed, and resulted in a six-to-three decision (with nine separate opinions) permitting publication. The decision generally stated that any prior restraint of the press bears "a heavy presumption against its constitutional validity"—without defining the type of evidence that would be necessary to justify prior restraint on national security grounds. In any case, it was not sufficient, the Court declared, for the executive branch to conclude that a need existed for prior restraint.

Although national security is hardly the concern when First Amendment issues are raised in the classroom, parallel considerations about societal order are raised. When they are in school, students do not receive the same level of constitutional protection that is accorded adults in the outside world. The issue was joined in a student protest against the same war that was at issue in the Pentagon Papers case. On December 16, 1965, thirteen-year-old Mary Beth Tinker, her brother, and a friend wore black armbands to their Des Moines, Iowa junior high school as a silent protest against the Vietnam War. When the students refused to remove the armbands, they were suspended. They brought suit to vindicate their First Amendment rights.

In *Tinker* v. *Des Moines Independent School District* (1969), Justice Abe Fortas delivered the Court's opinion in a seven-to-two decision, declaring that students do not "shed their constitutional rights to freedom of speech or expression at the schoolhouse gate." Noting that the silent protest caused no disorder or disturbance, Justice Fortas wrote that views that deviate from those of the majority "may start an argument or cause a disturbance [, b]ut our Constitution says we must take this risk." By not prohibiting all symbols of political or controversial significance, only these armbands, the school was attempting to control the content of speech, and that is impermissible.

A school board on Long Island, New York also crossed that line when it attempted to remove a number of books from the shelves of the school library. The controversy began after three board of education members attended a conference where they received a list of books considered objectionable by the meeting's politically conservative sponsors. The board then gave the school district an "unofficial direction" that ten books from the list be removed from its libraries until board members could read them. When the board's request received newspa-

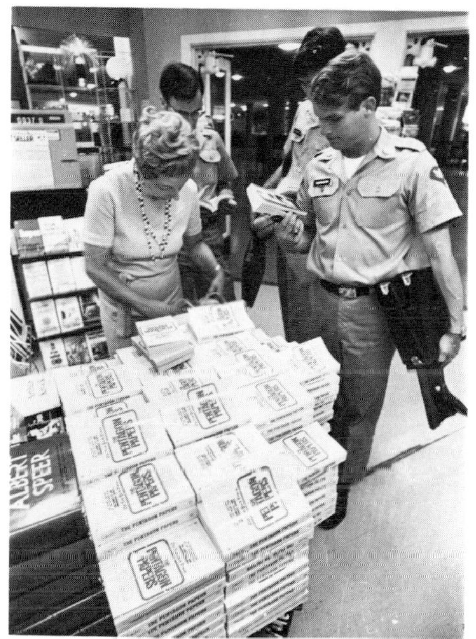

The Pentagon Papers on sale in paperback form at a bookstore in the shopping concourse at the Pentagon Building in Washington, D.C. One of the first customers for the book was the federal government, which took several hundred copies of the initial printing of 12,500 copies. 1971. AP/ Wide World Photos

Justice Abe Fortas. 1968. UPI/ Bettmann Newsphotos

Five students who brought suit with the New York Civil Liberties Union against the Island Tree Union Free School District No. 26, contesting the school board's action in banning several books from the school library.
AP/Wide World Photos

per attention, a press release was issued describing the books as "anti-American, anti-Christian, anti-Semitic, and just plain filthy."

Books such as *Slaughterhouse-Five* by Kurt Vonnegut, Jr., *The Naked Ape* by Desmond Morris, *Best Short Stories of Negro Writers*, edited by Langston Hughes, and *Soul on Ice*, by Eldridge Cleaver were on the list for removal. A review committee was appointed and recommended that five of the books be returned to the library, two be placed on restricted shelves, and two be removed entirely. The board rejected the recommendation, removing all but one book and giving no reason for its action.

Steven Pico and several fellow students filed a lawsuit claiming their First Amendment rights were violated by the book removals. By a five-to-four decision, with seven separate opinions, the Supreme Court upheld the students' right to pursue the lawsuit. Justice Brennan, speaking for the plurality decision in *Island Tree Union Free School District No. 26* v. *Pico* (1982), said that the school board acted unconstitutionally if it intended to deny the students "access to ideas with which [the board] disagreed." The Court majority condemned politically motivated book removals, but suggested that decisions based upon educational suitability could be upheld, especially when a regular system of review with standardized guidelines had been adopted.

Still, the Court has found justifiable limits to what students may say in a school setting. In *Bethel School District No. 403* v. *Fraser* (1986), Chief Justice Warren Burger declared it does not follow that "simply because the use of an offensive form of expression may not be prohibited to adults making what the speaker considers a political point, that the same latitude must be permitted to children in a public school."

Matthew N. Fraser, a high school student, was suspended for two days after making sexually suggestive remarks in a nominating speech for student office at a voluntary school assembly. Some students mimicked the sexual activities alluded to in the speech, while others "appeared bewildered and embarrassed." The Court found no free expression violation in Fraser's suspension.

"The undoubted freedom to advocate unpopular and controversial views in schools and classrooms," wrote Chief Justice Burger, "must be balanced against the society's countervailing interest in teaching students the boundaries of socially appropriate behavior. Even the most heated political discourse in a democratic society requires consideration for the personal sensibilities of the other participants and audiences."

The key to the decision was the lewd and indecent language used in the speech. The law in this area also has important implications for the kinds of books and other publications that may be used freely in the schools—an issue that is at the heart of the intermingling religious freedom and free expression issues present in cases appearing ever more frequently in the courts. The underlying value that must be upheld as these cases are decided was described succinctly by Justice Brennan:

> Our Nation is deeply committed to safeguarding academic freedom, which is of transcendent value to all of us and not merely to the teachers concerned. That freedom is therefore a special concern of the First Amendment, which does not tolerate laws that cast a pall of orthodoxy over the classroom. . . . The classroom is peculiarly the "marketplace of ideas." The Nation's future depends upon leaders trained through wide exposure to that robust exchange of ideas which discovers truth "out of a multitude of tongues, [rather] than through any kind of authoritative selection."

How the range of constitutional protections may accommodate the deeply held religious convictions of parents who object to the type of education their children may receive in the public schools, as well as the broad guarantee of free expression invoked by those who fear that the spectrum of knowledge will be constricted if the fundamentalists prevail, will ultimately be decided not in the courts, but through community consensus.

The Declaration of Independence. July 4, 1776. Library of Congress, Washington, D.C.

PART II

Judicial Power and Equality Under the Constitution

From the Declaration of Independence to the modern civil rights movement, the quest for equality has long been considered one of the most noble goals of the American Republic. The history of that quest, however, is filled not only with inspiring examples of heroism, but also with baser episodes that should not be forgotten lest they be repeated. The struggle has been and continues to be joined in every arena: the open forums favored by grass-roots political movements, the halls of our legislatures, the executive offices of our presidents and governors, as well as in courtrooms throughout the nation.

The courts have played a particularly important role in the quest for equality. It is little wonder that "I'll fight this all the way to the Supreme Court if I have to" is a familiar-sounding refrain. Throughout American history, citizens have sought judicial resolutions of their most nettlesome disputes. Today, the issues of equality most frequently brought before the courts stem from questions of education, housing, and employment.

In 1985, as a result of a lawsuit brought jointly by the Justice Department and the local branch of the National Association for the Advancement of Colored People (NAACP), federal Judge Leonard B. Sand ruled that Yonkers, New York—a half-urban, half-suburban city just north of New York City—had

Sketch by Cass Gilbert for his Supreme Court Building. 1928. Collection of the Supreme Court of the United States, Washington, D.C.

Justice William J. Brennan, Jr.'s opinion for the six-to-three decision in *Johnson* v. *Transportation Agency* (1987), noted that where there is "conspicuous imbalance in job categories traditionally segregated by race and sex" it is appropriate for public employers, as well as private, to take these factors into account when making hiring and promotion decisions. As a result of such successful litigation, as well as changes in social attitudes and perceptions, many women may now take advantage of job opportunities that were previously denied them. Reproduced with permission of AT&T Corporate Archive

John Jay by Gilbert Stuart and John Trumbull. 1804–1808. National Portrait Gallery, Smithsonian Institution, Washington, D.C.

"illegally and intentionally" segregated its schools and public housing by race. The six-hundred-page ruling was unique in linking education with housing in a desegregation case. In 1986, based upon a plan drawn up by Yonkers (New York State's fourth largest city), the judge ordered that attendance lines be redrawn for the 19,000-student school district that was roughly half white and half minority. In addition, he ordered the establishment of sixteen magnet schools and an extended day care program to allow parents to drop off and pick up their children outside of working hours. On housing, the judge ordered Yonkers to designate sites for 200 low-income housing units in mostly white residential areas and to create a fair housing office. Within the community—not unexpectedly—some citizens complained about the broad range of powers being exercised by a judge whose name many of them had never even heard before.

In San Francisco, two race and sex discrimination lawsuits have prevented the fire department from hiring any new firefighters for a five-year period. San Francisco has one of the country's only all-male fire departments, and eighty-five percent of its firefighters are white. Minority and female applicants went to court with charges of discrimination. While the lawsuit is pending, and with the parties unable to devise a mutually acceptable solution to the problem, federal Judge Marilyn H. Patel has enjoined the city from filling any vacancies. In the meantime, the city is struggling to maintain an effective department while remaining 170 firefighters short.

The Framers of the Constitution probably never envisioned that the courts would have such power over people's everyday lives or the operation of local government. *The Federalist*, eighty-five essays written to support the Constitution's ratification, is a still-relevant description of certain Framers' views—such as Alexander Hamilton's characterization of the judiciary as "least dangerous to the political rights of the constitution." For that assertion, Hamilton relied on the constitutional limitation that courts must hear "cases" or "controversies." They are not permitted to reach out to issues not properly placed before them. Thus, a federal court cannot pass on the constitutionality of legislation unless a litigant can claim that he is injured by it—not simply that he disagrees. The Supreme Court, under its first Chief Justice, John Jay, established this principle when it refused in 1790 to answer a request for an interpretation from then-Secretary of the Treasury Alexander Hamilton. The Court similarly rebuffed President George Washington in 1793, when he sought the Court's advice on the legal complexities stemming from his struggle to keep the new American nation neutral in the European war raging between England and France. The Chief Justice urged President Washington to "get that advice from the heads of the departments, that is the cabinet members." In each case, the Court's refusal was predicated upon the rule requiring it to deal with cases or controversies. The Supreme Court does not render advice.

The Court also does not address political questions—those issues more properly the province of the executive or the legislative branches. The Constitution's separation of powers provides the Court with its rationale for not invading the jurisdiction of the political branches. Another category of issues outside the purview of the judiciary are those that are not "justiciable"—problems for which there are no discoverable or manageable judicial standards by which they could be resolved.

But within the sphere of cases that are properly brought before it, the judicial branch is the ultimate authority, and the executive and legislature must defer to its interpretations. "The supremacy of the Constitution and the laws of the Union," James Madison observed, "without a supremacy in the exposition and execution of them will be as much a mockery as a scabbard in the hands of a soldier without a sword." The duty of explaining and interpreting the laws falls to the judiciary. This was perhaps one of the Constitution's most unique features: the establishment of a judiciary with final interpretative power, and independent of the political system. Justice Robert H. Jackson recognized the inherent difficulties in the Supreme Court's position when he wrote: "[W]e are not final because we are infallible, but we are infallible only because we are final."

The finality of Supreme Court decisions is subject, of course, to changes that may occur through constitutional amendment, or by changes in statutes that the Court has been asked to interpret. For example, the Sixteenth Amendment, authorizing the income tax, was a direct response to a Supreme Court decision finding an 1895 tax unconstitutional. And, of course, earlier decisions are sometimes reversed by later Courts whose members have reconsidered a constitutional question in the light of intervening experience and reflection. As Oliver Wendell Holmes, Jr. wrote in *The Common Law* (1881): "The life of the law has not been logic; it has been experience."

Alexander Hamilton, in *The Federalist* No. 78, envisioned ". . . the courts . . . as the bulwarks of a limited Constitution against legislative encroachments." He added: "The independence of the judges is equally requisite to guard the Constitution and the rights of individuals from the effects of those

The New York Merchants Exchange. The first terms of the Supreme Court of the United States were held here in 1790. Original Drawing, Emmet Collection, No. 1129. Courtesy of the Manuscript Division, The New York Public Library, Astor, Lenox and Tilden Foundations

Boston Daily Globe.

TRADITIONS VIOLATED.

Unprecedented Scene Enacted In the U S Supreme Court.

Justice Harlan in Dissenting From Opinion of Majority Declaring Income Tax Unconstitutional Was Deliberately Vehement.

ASSOCIATE JUSTICE HARLAN.

An article from the *Boston Daily Globe* recording Justice John Marshall Harlan's dissent from the majority opinion in the Supreme Court decision that declared the Income Tax unconstitutional. 1895. Harlan Papers, University of Louisville, Kentucky

This cartoon represents one view of President Franklin D. Roosevelt's "court-packing" plan. Collection of the Supreme Court of the United States, Washington, D.C.

The Supreme Court of the United States, 1986–1987. Standing, from left to right: Associate Justices Sandra Day O'Connor, Louis Franklin Powell, Jr., Thurgood Marshall, William Joseph Brennan, Jr., Chief Justice William Hubbs Rehnquist, Associate Justices Byron Raymond White, Harry A. Blackmun, John Paul Stevens, Antonin Scalia. Collection of the Supreme Court of the United States, Washington, D.C.

ill humours [of the majority]."

The Constitution provides the barest outlines of the judicial branch, much less than for either the legislature or the executive. Instead, it was left to Congress to work out the details, which it first did in the Judiciary Act of 1789. For example, the Constitution does not mandate the number of Justices on the Supreme Court. The original Court was established with six members. Although its number once reached ten, today's Court has nine Justices.

Congress also can and has made changes in the Court's jurisdiction. In the early years of the Union, after the Republicans had captured control of the presidency, as well as of the Congress, they passed legislation of questionable constitutionality. To prevent the Court from hearing a challenge to the law until the new administration had settled in, Congress eliminated the Supreme Court's 1802 term, and thus the Court did not meet from December 1801 until February 1803. Congress similarly repealed a preexisting grant of jurisdiction after a constitutional challenge to the Reconstruction Acts, passed after the Civil War, had been argued before the Court—although a decision had not yet been announced. In *Ex parte McCardle* (1869), the Court upheld Congress's authority to control its jurisdiction in that instance. However, in 1962, Justices William O. Douglas and Hugo L. Black questioned whether the *McCardle* principle would be upheld by a modern Court.

It is not surprising that the courts are embroiled in the most worrisome of contemporary issues. We look to the judiciary to reconcile diverse objectives that sometimes threaten to pull apart our constitutional seams. Occasionally, this requires the courts to invalidate actions of the other branches. Nowhere in the Constitution is this power of "judicial review" specifically established. The concept had its roots in English common law. Chief Justice Coke in *Bonham's Case* (1610) declared, "when an act of Parliament is against common right and reason . . . the common law will control it and adjudge such act to be void." Coke's approach had obvious appeal in the American colonies; it became a legal justification against the parliamentary enactments that later led to the Revolution.

After independence had been won, the principle of judicial review found support in the decisions of the early state courts, in *The Federalist* No. 78, and in *Hayburn's Case* (1792). It received its most sweeping enunciation in Chief Justice John Marshall's opinion in *Marbury* v. *Madison* (1803)—a case stemming from efforts on the part of John Adams to ensure that the Federalists would continue to control the judiciary after he left office. President Adams had created a number of judgeships that were pushed through Congress on the eve of Thomas Jef-

Caricature on Reconstruction. 1865. The New-York Historical Society

Edward Coke. 1592. Department of the Environment, London. British Crown Copyright. Reproduced with the permission of the Controller of Her Britannic Majesty's Stationery Office and the Advisory Committee on Works of Art in the House of Commons

Chief Justice John Marshall

Caricature on the comparative virtues of George Washington and Thomas Jefferson. 1807. The New-York Historical Society

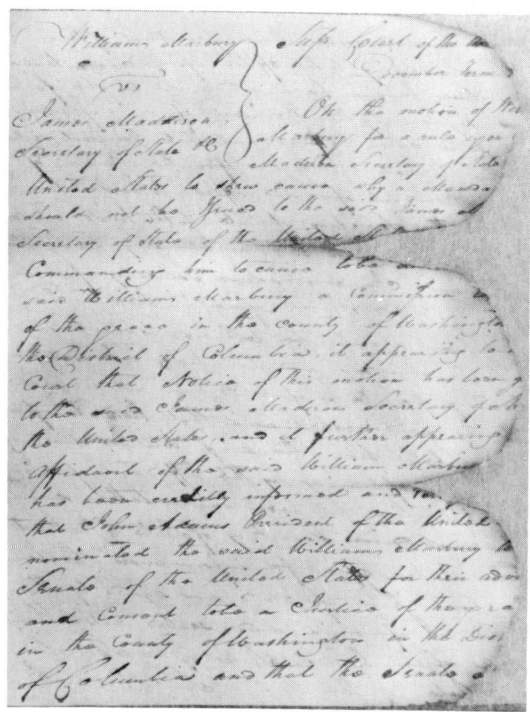

William Marbury
vs
James Madison Secretary of State &c
Sup. Court of the U.S.
December term

On the motion of Wm
Marbury for a rule upon
Madison Secretary of State
United States to shew cause why a Mandamus
should not be issued to the said James as
Secretary of State of the United St
Commanding him to cause to be
said William Marbury a Commission
of the peace in the County of Washington
the District of Columbia, it appearing to
Court that Notice of this motion has been
to the said James Madison Secretary of
the United States, and it further appearing
Affidavit of the said William Marbury
has been credibly informed and
that John Adams President of the United
nominated the said William Marbury to
Senate of the United States for their advice
and Consent to be a Justice of the peace
in the County of Washington in the Dist
of Columbia and that the Senate

Show-cause order filed by William Marbury, and served on James Madison. 1801. Damaged in the Capitol fire of 1898. Photograph by Jonathan Wallen. National Archives, Washington, D.C.

John Marshall by William James Hubard. 1832. An interesting character study in contrast to earlier portraits. National Portrait Gallery, Smithsonian Institution, Washington, D.C.

ferson's presidential inauguration. Among these "midnight judges" was William Marbury, who had been appointed a justice of the peace. When he took office, President Jefferson ordered his Secretary of State, James Madison, to withhold a number of the last-minute commissions, including Marbury's, that had not yet been delivered. Marbury and several others sought a writ of mandamus—a court order requiring Madison to deliver the commissions in question.

While the battle over the commission was obviously important to Marbury, broader issues were at stake. Jefferson's succession to the presidency and his party's newly established control of Congress was a significant event, since it marked the first peaceful transfer of power from one political party to another in this country. At the same time, it marked the first instance of divided government—the Supreme Court bench was filled with Federalists, while the other branches were in Republican hands. On a more personal level, there was the rivalry and strong feelings of animosity between two cousins, Republican President Thomas Jefferson and Federalist Chief Justice John Marshall. Also at stake was the Supreme Court's future role in the rough and tumble world of government—the decision in *Marbury* v. *Madison* would thrust the Court into open assumption of its role as the head of a fully coequal branch of government.

Chief Justice Marshall's opinion in the case was brilliant in its resolution of the complex political issues, even if he also had to deal rather deftly with precedent, history, and logic in the process. He gave the Jeffersonians the victory they sought—the denial of Marbury's commission—while simultaneously establishing the Supreme Court's authority to review acts of Congress and presidential initiatives. In essence, the decision held that "an act of the legislature, repugnant to the constitution, is void." The law in question here was a section of the 1789 Judiciary Act that purported to allow cases for a writ of mandamus to be initiated in the Supreme Court, rather than beginning at a lower-level court. This, Marshall said, was beyond the authority of Congress to grant, since the Constitution was the only source of the Court's original jurisdiction, and the Constitution said that such cases could be brought before the Supreme Court only on appeal.

Although that decision, one of the Court's first written opinions (opinions had been delivered orally from the bench), seemingly established the validity of judicial review, that power has remained a central issue in constitutional debates. It is often the courts alone that stand between a validly enacted statute and its acceptance as law. Still, the courts generally exercise this power sparingly and avoid constitutional questions

RICHARD III.

Andrew Jackson, caricatured here as Richard III in 1836, had ignored the Supreme Court's decision in *Worcester* v. *Georgia* (1832), which denied state authority to pass any laws affecting the Cherokees. Chief Justice John Marshall's ruling held that the federal government had exclusive jurisdiction over Indian affairs. President Jackson supposedly said: "John Marshall has made his decision; now let him enforce it." The New-York Historical Society

Draft of the Declaration of Independence. 1776. Library of Congress, Washington, D.C.

BY

HEWLETT & BRIGHT.

SALE OF

VALUABLE SLAVES,

(On account of departure)

The Owner of the following named and valuable Slaves, being on the eve of departure for Europe, will cause the same to be offered for sale, at the NEW EXCHANGE, corner of St. Louis and Chartres streets, on *Saturday*, May 16, at Twelve o'Clock, *viz.*

1. SARAH, a mulatress, aged 45 years, a good cook and accustomed to house work in general, is an excellent and faithful nurse for sick persons, and in every respect a first rate character.

2. DENNIS, her son, a mulatto, aged 24 years, a first rate cook and stew-ard for a vessel, having been in that capacity for many years on board one of the Mobile packets; is strictly honest, temperate, and a first rate subject.

3. CHOLE, a mulatress, aged 36 years, she is, without exception, one of the most competent servants in the country, a first rate washer and ironer, does up lace, a good cook, and for a bachelor who wishes a house-keeper she would be invaluable; she is also a good ladies' maid, having travelled to the North in that capacity.

4. FANNY, her daughter, a mulatress, aged 16 years, speaks French and English, is a superior hair-dresser, (pupil of Guilliac,) a good seamstress and ladies' maid, is smart, intelligent, and a first rate character.

5. DANDRIDGE, a mulatoo, aged 26 years, a first rate dining-room ser-vant, a good painter and rough carpenter, and has but few equals for honesty and sobriety.

6. NANCY, his wife, aged about 24 years, a confidential house servant, good seamstress, mantuamaker and tailoress, a good cook, washer and ironer, etc.

7. MARY ANN, her child, a creole, aged 7 years, speaks French and English, is smart, active and intelligent.

8. FANNY or FRANCES, a mulatress, aged 22 years, is a first rate washer and ironer, good cook and house servant, and has an excellent character.

9. EMMA, an orphan, aged 10 or 11 years, speaks French and English, has been in the country 7 years, has been accustomed to waiting on table, sewing etc.; is intelligent and active.

10. FRANK, a mulatto, aged about 32 years speaks French and English, is a first rate hostler and coachman, understands perfectly well the management of horses, and is, in every respect, a first rate character, with the exception that he will occasionally drink, though not an habitual drunkard.

☞ All the above named Slaves are acclimated and excellent subjects; they were purchased by their present vendor many years ago, and will, therefore, be severally warranted against all vices and maladies prescribed by law, save and except FRANK, who is fully guaranteed in every other respect but the one above mentioned.

TERMS:—One-half Cash, and the other half in notes at Six months, drawn and endorsed to the satisfaction of the Vendor, with special mortgage on the Slaves until final payment. The Acts of Sale to be passed before WILLIAM BOSWELL, *Notary Public*, at the expense of the Purchaser.

***New-Orleans, May* 13, 1835.**

PRINTED BY BENJAMIN LEVY.

A handbill concerning the sale of slaves, describing their virtues and accomplishments. 1835. The New-York Historical Society

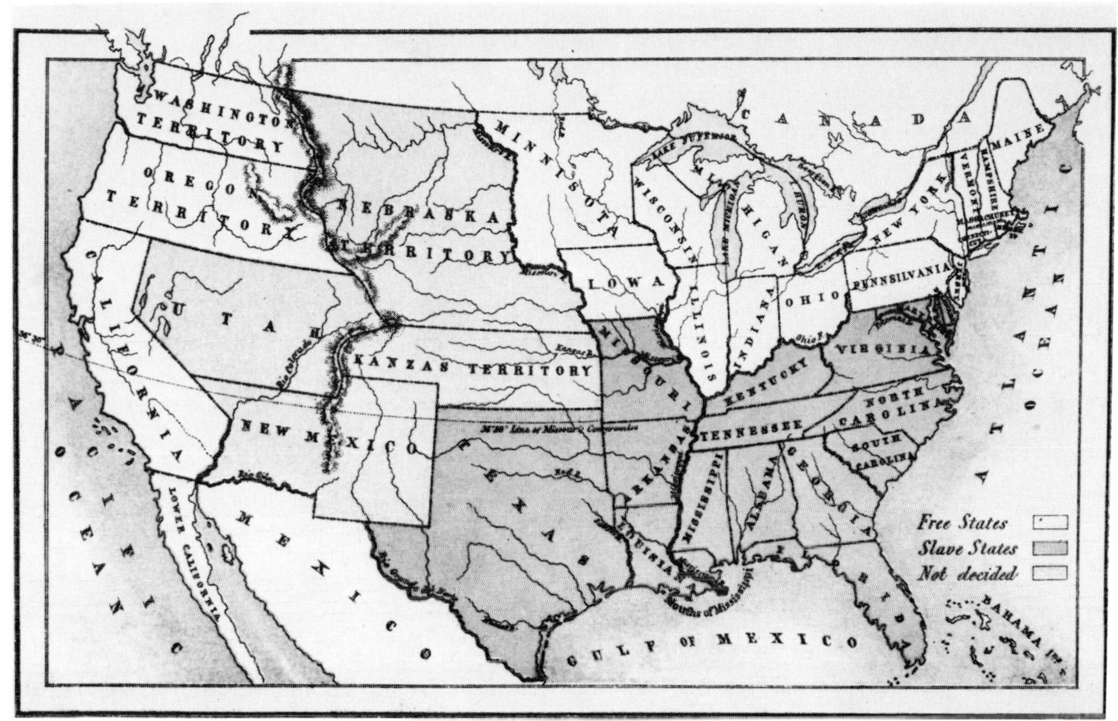

Map showing "Free States, Slave States, and Not decided," Published in England, 1857. The Historic New Orleans Collection

if there are any other grounds upon which their decisions may rest. It was more than fifty years after *Marbury* v. *Madison* before the Supreme Court invalidated another act of Congress—slavery would then be the issue.

The institution of slavery was an original sin for which we are still paying the price. Slavery was so much a part of American colonial life that a reference to it as a violation of the "sacred rights of life and liberty" was quickly deleted from Thomas Jefferson's original draft of the Declaration of Independence, while the Second Continental Congress basked in the glory of the phrase, "all men are created equal," without noting any contradiction.

Slavery was also very much a regional issue. It was relatively easy for the commercial and industrial North (where slavery was still widespread but of little economic consequence) to take the high moral ground, but the South was heavily dependent upon continued slave imports for its labor-intensive and agricultural economy. Fifteen of the delegates to the Constitutional Convention are known to have owned slaves, while only Benjamin Franklin and Alexander Hamilton could fairly be characterized as abolitionists. Several northern delegates, and George Mason of Virginia, objected to protecting slavery in the Constitution, but did not press the issue after the Carolinas and Georgia threatened to abandon the Union "unless their right to import slaves be untouched." Some del-

George Mason, the author of the Virginia Bill of Rights of 1776, also drafted the proposals for a Federal Bill of Rights adopted by the Virginia convention that ratified the Constitution in 1788. Courtesy Virginia State Library, Richmond

The Underground Railway by Charles T. Webber. Ac. #1927.26. The Cincinnati Museum Association egates consoled themselves with the rationale that it was more appropriate to deal with the issue on a states' rights basis—let each state decide for itself whether to be free or slave.

Using the euphemisms "other persons" or "such persons" to refer to slaves, the Constitution gave nodding approval to slavery, leading abolitionist William Lloyd Garrison and the Massachusetts Anti-Slavery Society to later call it a "covenant with death and an agreement with hell." Constitutional provisions prevented Congress from prohibiting the slave trade before 1808. When the South pressed to have slaves included in the census to bolster its representation in Congress, the three-fifths compromise was adopted, seeming to render a slave as less than a whole person.

Slavery remained controversial during the nation's early years, fueled by incidents such as the slave uprising led by Nat Turner in 1831. Garrison's *Liberator* was not a very influential periodical, but it did help to launch a militant abolitionist movement that reached its apogee with John Brown's 1859 raid on Harper's Ferry. A new body of literature sprang up around the issue, with Harriet Beecher Stowe's *Uncle Tom's Cabin* (1852) becoming the best known of the anti-slavery tracts.

The compromises concerning slavery made at the Constitutional Convention provided the model for future compromises. The free state of California was admitted to the Union only when balanced by concessions to the South that included a stronger fugitive-slave law and establishment of the New Mexico and Utah Territories without any restrictions as to slavery. This Compromise of 1850 did not lessen tensions, however, and Kansas soon became a battleground over slavery. It was then that the case of Dred Scott, an uneducated slave from Missouri, captured the nation's attention.

In Missouri, Dred Scott had been the property of a family named Blow, who sold Scott to Dr. John Emerson, an army surgeon later posted to Illinois, a state that prohibited slavery, and to the free Wisconsin Territory. During these postings, Scott accompanied Emerson as a body servant, returning with the doctor to Missouri in 1838. After Dr. Emerson's death, his widow moved to New York, delegating Scott's care to the Blow family, his original owners. Harry Blow, a young lawyer strongly opposed to slavery, sought to gain Dred Scott's freedom by initiating a suit in the Missouri courts that began as *Scott, a Man of Color* v. *Emerson*, and was based upon the ground that Scott's years of residence on free soil had made *him* free. Of course, Scott's owner, Mrs. Emerson, could have freed him at any time, but she sympathized with Blow's ideals, and agreed to become the defendant of record in the case in order to seek a broader forum for the fight against slavery.

H.T. Blow. 1817–1875. The Missouri Historical Society

After six years of litigation, the Missouri supreme court ruled that Scott's status was controlled by Missouri law and he must remain a slave. But now the case took a new twist. Scott's owner of record, Mrs. Emerson, supposedly sold Scott to her brother, John F. A. Sanford of New York, and the case was revived in 1854 in the federal circuit court for Missouri as *Dred Scott* v. *Sandford* (sic). Because the circuit court was persuaded to rule that it lacked jurisdiction, the lawyers for Scott were able to appeal directly to the Supreme Court on a writ of error, and the case was ultimately decided in 1857, with Chief Justice Roger B. Taney delivering the Court's opinion.

The Supreme Court's ruling was that Scott remained a slave and had no standing to sue, since slaves were not citizens. Citing one law after another, Chief Justice Taney detailed white America's racial attitudes before, during, and after the Revolution, concluding that the Framers were in agreement that even free blacks "had no rights which the white man was bound to respect; and that the Negro might justly and lawfully be reduced to slavery for his benefit." The Chief Justice pointed to the two provisions in the Constitution that dealt with slavery, emphasizing that both "treat them [slaves] as property and make it the duty of the government to protect it." Since Scott was property, the character of property could not be changed by passing through another state or territory.

But the opinion went even further, declaring that the Missouri Compromise of 1820, which had divided the Louisiana Purchase into free and slave sections—and designated the Wisconsin Territory as part of the free section—was unconstitutional. According to Taney's findings, the Constitution provided the Congress with no authority to forbid slavery in the new territory.

The *Dred Scott* decision brought a fire storm of protest and helped to make slavery the dominant issue in the 1860 presidential race. Abraham Lincoln's election was followed by the Southern states' secession from the Union, and the Civil War. Although the war began solely to preserve the Union, an end to slavery was eventually incorporated into its objectives. Lincoln's Emancipation Proclamation, even if it had no legal force, was of enormous symbolic importance and laid the groundwork for the Thirteenth Amendment, which abolished slavery in 1865. Then, in 1870, the Fifteenth Amendment granted the former slaves the right to vote (a right that would not be truly realized until the 1960s, with the abolition of the poll tax by constitutional amendment, the Supreme Court's reapportionment decisions, and the Voting Rights Act of 1965). Freedom for the slaves, however, did not mean true equality, since the newly emancipated blacks remained poor, uneducated, and

View of St. Louis, 1854, showing the domed courthouse that was the first venue for the case which became *Dred Scott* v. *Sandford*. The building is still in use. The Missouri Historical Society

Chief Justice Roger B. Taney. Library of Congress, Washington, D.C.

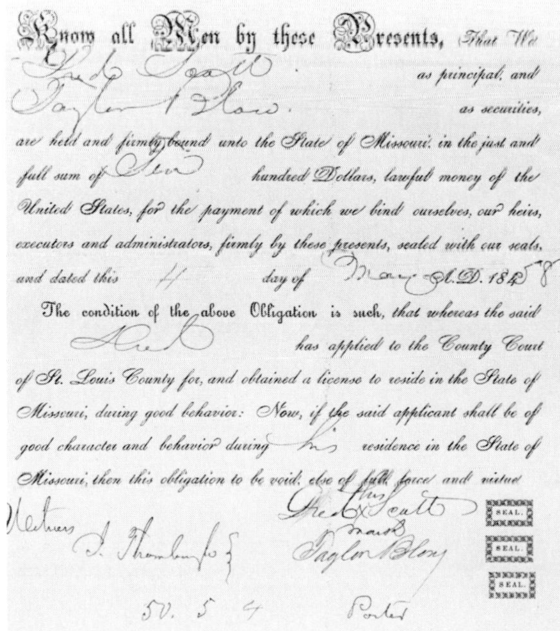

Know all Men by these Presents, That We [illegible] as principal, and [illegible] as securities, are held and firmly bound unto the State of Missouri, in the just and full sum of [illegible] hundred Dollars, lawful money of the United States, for the payment of which we bind ourselves, our heirs, executors and administrators, firmly by these presents, sealed with our seals, and dated this 4 day of May A.D. 1858

The condition of the above Obligation is such, that whereas the said [illegible] has applied to the County Court of St. Louis County for, and obtained a license to reside in the State of Missouri, during good behavior: Now, if the said applicant shall be of good character and behavior during his residence in the State of Missouri, then this obligation to be void, else of full force and virtue

Witness [illegible] — Dred X Scott (his mark) SEAL.

Taylor Blow SEAL.

SEAL.

50. 5 4 Porter

Slave Bond of Dred Scott. The Missouri Historical Society

Abraham Lincoln. May 7, 1858. The University Libraries, University of Nebraska-Lincoln

Ku Klux Klan, Alabama, 1868. *Carte de visite* photograph, 3 1/4 x 2 1/2″. Rutherford B. Hayes Presidential Center, Freemont, Ohio

Caricature by Thomas Nast. 1868. "This is a white man's government." "We regard the Reconstruction Acts (so called) of Congress as usurpations, and unconstitutional, revolutionary, and void."—Democratic Platform. The New-York Historical Society

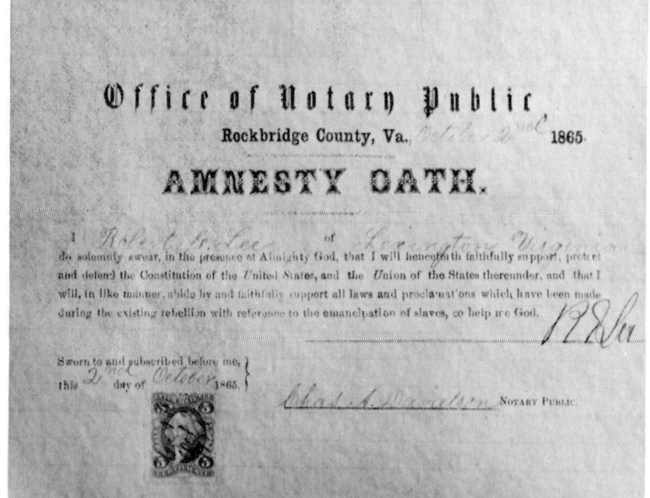

Office of Notary Public

Rockbridge County, Va., October 2nd 1865

AMNESTY OATH.

I Robert E. Lee of Lexington Virginia do solemnly swear, in the presence of Almighty God, that I will henceforth faithfully support, protect and defend the Constitution of the United States, and the Union of the States thereunder, and that I will, in like manner, abide by and faithfully support all laws and proclamations which have been made during the existing rebellion with reference to the emancipation of slaves, so help me God.

R E Lee

Sworn to and subscribed before me, this 2nd day of October 1865.

Chas. A. Davidson Notary Public

Amnesty Oath of Robert E. Lee. 1865. National Archives, Washington, D.C.

In the House of Representatives.

December 4, 1865.

On motion of Mr. Stevens:

Be it resolved, by the Senate and House of Representatives in Congress assembled: That a joint committee of fifteen members shall be appointed, nine of whom shall be members of the House, and six members of the Senate, who shall enquire into the condition of the States which formed the so-called Confederate States of America, and report whether they, or any of them, are entitled to be represented in either House of Congress, with leave to report at any time, by bill or otherwise; and until such report shall have been made, and finally acted on by Congress, no member shall be received into either House from any of the so-called Confederate States; and all papers relating to the representation of said States shall be referred to the said Committee without debate.

Attest

Edw'd. McPherson, Clerk.

December 13, 1865.

Amended in the Senate, on motion of Mr. Anthony, so as to read,

Resolved by the House of Representatives, (the Senate concurring) That a joint committee of fifteen members shall be appointed, nine of whom shall be members of the House, and six members of the Senate, who shall enquire into the condition of the States which formed the so-called Confederate States of America, and report whether they, or any of them, are entitled to be represented in either House of Congress, with leave to report at any time, by bill or otherwise.

441835

First page of the Journal of the Joint Committee on Reconstruction, Thirty-Ninth Congress, First Session. 1865. Rare Book and Manuscript Collection. Columbia University Library, New York concentrated in the South, where cultural barriers—as oppressive as legal ones—remained in force.

Of all the post-Civil War constitutional changes, the Fourteenth Amendment (the text most frequently cited in today's civil rights cases) was the most far-reaching. It fundamentally changed the relationship of the states to the federal government and introduced a particular concept of equality into the Constitution. The former Confederate states were re-admitted to the Union on the condition that they ratify the Fourteenth Amendment. As a result, the Reconstruction legislatures of the South gave their unanimous approval to the Amendment, while the Northern states summoned just that three-fourths approval necessary for ratification in 1868.

The Fourteenth Amendment nationalized citizenship, previously a creature of the states alone, and voided the three-fifths language concerning the way in which representation in Congress had been determined. It also prohibited the states from interfering with the "privileges or immunities" of United States citizens. This prohibition did not seem to sway the Supreme Court in deciding the *Slaughterhouse Cases* (1873), where a distinction between national and state citizenship was drawn. These cases involved a group of New Orleans butchers who claimed that the establishment of a city-sanctioned monopoly eliminated their businesses and violated their citizenship rights. The Court decided that no national citizenship rights were violated, and that the Constitution afforded the complainants no relief for the violation, if any, of state citizenship rights. Although not involved in these specific cases, blacks suffered a major setback as a result of the decision, since most of the privileges of citizenship were of a state—not a national—nature.

The Fourteenth Amendment also contained other important provisions. It made the Constitution's guarantee of due process—previously applicable to the federal government alone—binding upon the states. It was not until the landmark decisions handed down by the Warren Court in the 1950s and 1960s, however, that this provision would become fully operative. Finally, in the area of modern concerns, the Amendment guaranteed all individuals "equal protection of the laws."

For a time, Supreme Court decisions continued to evidence hostility to the Reconstruction-era amendments. In 1875, Congress passed a Civil Rights Act, purporting to enforce the Fourteenth Amendment's provisions by making it a punishable offense to deny anyone "equal accommodations and privileges in all inns, public conveyances and places of public amusement." If that Act had been put into effect, the upheavals of the civil rights movement in the 1950s and 1960s

The Warren Court is often described as an "activist" Supreme Court. However, perhaps one of the most activist records belonged to the Hughes Court—characterized as the "Nine Old Men"—whose majority's conservative views ran counter to the economic regulations that were part of the "New Deal." Caricature by Al Hirschfeld. The "Nine Old Men" of the Supreme Court. 1937. From left to right: Associate Justices Owen J. Roberts, Pierce Butler, Louis D. Brandeis, Willis Van Devanter, Chief Justice Charles Evans Hughes, Associate Justices James C. McReynolds, George Sutherland, Harlan Fiske Stone, and Benjamin N. Cardozo. Franklin D. Roosevelt Library

Justice Joseph P. Bradley. Collection of the Supreme Court of the United States, Washington, D.C.

As this 1949 photograph illustrates, separate seating was maintained in public transportation throughout the South long after *Plessy* v. *Ferguson* (1896). Courtesy, The Historic New Orleans Collection, Museum/Research Center might never have occurred, but the Supreme Court found the statute unconstitutional in the *Civil Rights Cases* (1883). The ruling denied that Congress had any power to protect individual rights as a result of the Constitution's grant that the legislature may "enforce, by appropriate legislation, the provisions" of the Fourteenth Amendment. Justice Joseph P. Bradley's opinion also denied that the type of discrimination that the Civil Rights Act was intended to prevent was a "badge of slavery" prohibited by the Thirteenth Amendment. The decision drew a vigorous dissent from Justice John Marshall Harlan for being "narrow and artificial." Justice Harlan also disagreed in another great civil rights case, *Plessy* v. *Ferguson* (1896), and his lone dissent was not only prophetic, but would be vindicated in the 1954 landmark decision, *Brown* v. *Board of Education of Topeka*.

Homer Adolph Plessy was one-eighth black, seven-eighths white. He had purchased a first-class ticket on a Louisiana railroad, but was denied seating in the section reserved for whites. After refusing to move to the "colored coach," he was arrested under a state "Jim Crow" statute authorizing this segregation. Justice Henry B. Brown wrote the majority opinion for the Supreme Court, finding that the Fourteenth Amendment's goal "was undoubtedly to enforce the absolute equality of the two races before the law, but in the nature of things it could not have been intended to abolish distinctions based upon color, or to enforce social, as distinguished from political equality, or a commingling of the two races upon terms unsatisfactory to either."

Justice Harlan's dissent was clear and unequivocal: "In the view of the Constitution, in the eye of the law, there is in this country no superior, dominant, ruling class of citizens. There is no caste here. Our Constitution is color-blind, and neither knows nor tolerates classes among citizens."

Not all of the Supreme Court's decisions concerning racial questions, however, sanctioned discrimination. One significant case, *Yick Wo* v. *Hopkins* (1886), had its humble beginnings in a Chinese laundry that was little more than a wooden shed. A new San Francisco ordinance, ostensibly for health and safety reasons, required the consent of the city's supervisors for any laundry operation, unless it was housed in a brick or stone building. Lee Yick, a Chinese alien who had operated a laundry in that city for twenty-two years and had obtained health and fire certificates, was subsequently denied permission to continue in business, then arrested along with more than 150 other operators of Chinese laundries in wooden structures. All but ten of the city's 320 laundries were housed in wooden premises; 240 of these were owned by Chinese operators. The

Justice John Marshall Harlan.
Collection of the Supreme Court of the United States, Washington, D.C.

Justice Stanley Matthews. Library of Congress, Washington, D.C.

Segregated waiting rooms at the railroad depot in Jackson, Mississippi. 1956. AP/Wide World Photos

ordinance was invoked only against the Chinese.

The Supreme Court found the ordinance's administration a denial of equal protection of the laws. As Justice Stanley Matthews wrote: "Though the law itself be fair on its face and impartial in appearance, yet, if it is applied and administered by public authority with an evil eye and an unequal hand, so as practically to make unjust and illegal discriminations between persons in similar circumstances, material to their rights, the denial of equal justice is still within the prohibition of the Constitution."

The *Yick Wo* v. *Hopkins* decision established that discriminatory effect was as repugnant to the Constitution as direct discrimination. Sporadically, the Court began to recognize the promise that equal protection was meant to establish. In 1917, for example, it struck down a Louisville, Kentucky ordinance preventing blacks from moving into white neighborhoods. In 1938, a qualified black law school applicant was found to have been denied his rights when Missouri sought to send him out-of-state rather than admit him to the all-white state law school. Similarly, in *Sweatt* v. *Painter* (1950), the University of Texas Law School was required to admit a black applicant because the "black school" operated by the state failed to offer substantially equal educational opportunities.

World War II provided many white soldiers with their first close contacts with blacks, although units remained segregated. The war also introduced a bleak chapter into American history as many Japanese-Americans were rounded up and placed in guarded camps. Fear of espionage by those of Japanese ancestry led the Supreme Court, by a six-to-three vote, to validate this treatment in *Korematsu* v. *United States* (1944). Fred Korematsu was arrested for remaining in a public area designated a "military zone" to which only Japanese-Americans were denied entry. The Supreme Court upheld his conviction. In 1983—nearly forty years later—Korematsu's conviction was overturned because the government had knowingly withheld evidence about the military necessity of the zone. Judge Marilyn H. Patel, the presiding judge in the San Francisco firefighters' case described at the beginning of this section, added that though the *Korematsu* decision was never explicitly reversed, it "lies overruled in the court of history."

One aspect of the decision, however, established a still-valid standard of analyzing equal protection claims. Justice Hugo L. Black wrote: "It should be noted . . . that all legal restrictions which curtail the civil rights of a single racial group are immediately suspect. . . . [C]ourts must subject them to the most rigid scrutiny. Pressing public necessity may sometimes justify the existence of such restrictions; racial antago-

After the outbreak of war with Japan, the United States Government began moving Japanese living in what were characterized as "vital coastal and defense areas" into inland "Reception Centers." In this March 1942 photo, a first contingent of Japanese technicians—doctors, nurses, clerks, and stenographers—is shown as they prepared to leave Los Angeles in three buses and under Army escort, to establish a "Reception Center" at Manzanar, California. UPI/Bettmann Newsphotos

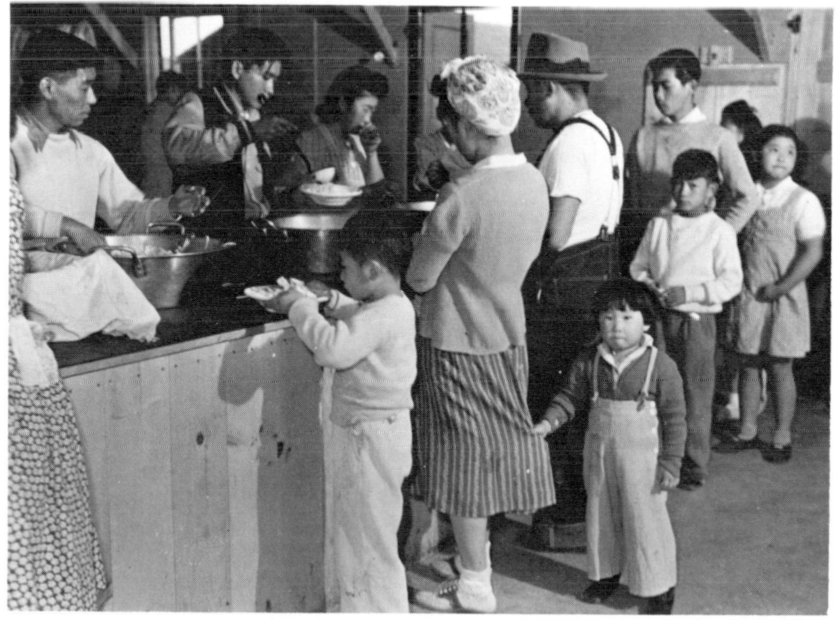

Dinner being served cafeteria style in the Mess Halls at the Heart Mountain "Relocation Center" in Colorado where Japanese from California had been sent "for the duration." 1943. UPI/Bettmann Newsphotos

Justice Hugo Black, Mrs. Black, and Senator Sherman Minton of Indiana, at a concert given by Marian Anderson on the steps of the Lincoln Memorial. 1939. UPI/Bettmann Newsphotos

Thurgood Marshall and Mrs. Marshall, at the Senate Judiciary Committee hearings concerning Mr. Marshall's appointment as an Associate Justice of the Supreme Court. During this session, Senator Sam Ervin, Jr. (Democrat-North Carolina), spoke out at length against Supreme Court rulings on civil rights, voluntary confessions, and right to counsel. 1967. UPI/Bettmann Newsphotos

The former Linda Brown, now Mrs. Charles P. Smith, is shown here in front of Sumner School in Topeka, Kansas. Refusal of this school to admit Linda, then nine, in 1951, led to the suit whose name was given to several cases which reached the Supreme Court, and in turn to the Court's historic decision against school segregation in 1954. The decision came too late for Linda, but her two sisters attended Sumner School. 1964. AP/Wide World Photos

The Vinson Court. 1949–1953. Standing, from left: Associate Justices Tom Campbell Clark, Robert Hougwout Jackson, Harold Hitz Burton, Sherman Minton. Seated, from left: Associate Justices Felix Frankfurter, Hugo Lafayette Black, Chief Justice Frederick Moore Vinson, Associate Justices Stanley Forman Reed, William Orville Douglas. Photograph by Fabian Bachrach. Collection of the Supreme Court of the United States, Washington, D.C.

nism never can."

That strict standard must have encouraged stategists at the NAACP Legal Defense and Educational Fund who were searching for a way to attack the constitutionality of racial segregation—especially in the schools. Led by Thurgood Marshall (who would become the first black Supreme Court Justice in 1967), the Fund successfully challenged segregation at the college level. It then turned its attention toward reversing the *Plessy* v. *Ferguson* approval of the "separate, but equal" approach. The perfect vehicle for this attempt appeared in four cases from Delaware, Kansas, South Carolina, and Virginia that were grouped together and reached the Supreme Court as *Brown* v. *Board of Education of Topeka* (1954).

Linda Brown was a third-grade student in Topeka, Kansas who attended the all-black Monroe School some distance from her home. To get there, she had to walk several blocks through a railroad yard to a place where she could catch a school bus. She had to leave home at 7:40 A.M. to reach the Monroe School at 9:00 A.M. After receiving a notice for the all-white neighborhood school, her father, Oliver, tried in vain to register her there.

The case reached the Supreme Court for argument in 1952 and, at the Court's request, it was reargued in 1953. The postponement of the decision had an unexpected effect on the final decision. Chief Justice Fred M. Vinson, who had indicated to his fellow Justices that he was not prepared to overrule

Chief Justice Fred M. Vinson and President Harry S Truman, enroute to the Army-Navy Game at Philadelphia, November 27, 1948. Vinson Papers, University of Kentucky

The three lawyers who participated in arguments before the Supreme Court in the school desegregation cases (*Brown* v. *Board of Education of Topeka*, 1954), are shown here during a recess of the hearing. Left to right: John W. Davis of New York, chief representative of the states defending segregation, J.L. Rankin, Assistant United States Attorney for the Federal Government, and Thurgood Marshall of New York, chief counsel for the NAACP Legal Defense Fund. UPI/Bettmann Archive

Plessy, died suddenly, and Governor Earl Warren of California was named to replace him. The possibility of a badly split decision in favor of the *Brown* plaintiffs evolved instead into a unanimous decision under the skillful leadership of Chief Justice Warren.

The stakes were so high in this case that South Carolina was represented by John W. Davis, the 1928 Democratic presidential candidate, who was considered by many to be the nation's best appellate attorney. Rising to meet the challenge, Thurgood Marshall argued that the only grounds upon which a color barrier could be maintained would be "an inherent determination that the people who were formerly in slavery regardless of anything else, shall be kept as near that stage as is possible, and now is the time, we submit, that this Court should make it clear that that is not what our Constitution stands for."

Chief Justice Warren conducted a full discussion of the case in conference with the other Justices, but asked that it be done without taking any vote—an unusual step. At the end of the discussion, Warren indicated "my instincts and feelings lead me to say that, in these cases, we should abolish the practice of segregation in the public schools—but in a tolerant way." Warren's approach was correctly calculated to win support for overruling *Plessy*. He thought he could command a majority but wished to forestall the possibility of dissenting or concurring opinions that might weaken the moral authority of that decision. He succeeded in winning agreement to a single, unanimous opinion which he would write and deliver.

Noting the central importance of public education to American society and individual success in life, Chief Justice Warren wrote simply but powerfully: "We conclude that in the field of public education the doctrine of 'separate but equal' has no place. Separate educational facilities are inherently unequal." However, to devise an effective remedy for so complex an issue, the Court scheduled a new argument for the following term.

The *Brown* decision produced what Justice Hugo Black called "a storm over this Court." Senator James O. Eastland of Mississippi accused the Justices of invading a sphere reserved by the Constitution to the states, and to another branch of government at that. The South, he said, "will not abide by or obey this legislative decision by a political court." The mounting pressure on the Court was tremendous. Even President Dwight D. Eisenhower, at a state dinner where Earl Warren was purposely seated near losing advocate Davis, took the Chief Justice aside to offer an extralegal argument on behalf of the South, based upon his view of Southern sensitivities to the

Integration, Supreme Court by Ben Shahn. 1963. A painting of the 1953–1954 Warren Court. Des Moines Art Center. James D. Edmundson Purchase Fund

The Warren Court that decided *Brown* v. *Board of Education of Topeka*, 1953–1955. Standing, from left: Associate Justices Tom Campbell Clark, Robert Hougwout Jackson, Harold Hitz Burton, Sherman Minton. Seated, from left: Associate Justices Felix Frankfurter, Hugo Lafayette Black, Chief Justice Earl Warren, Associate Justices Stanley Forman Reed, William Orville Douglas. Photograph by Ackad, Washington, D.C. Collection of the Supreme Court of the United States, Washington, D.C.

realities of school integration.

In *Brown II*, the Court dealt with the need for a remedy, fully aware that their decree would face resistance in the South. The Court sent the four cases that had been consolidated under *Brown* back to the lower courts with instructions that blacks were to be admitted to schools on a nondiscriminatory basis "with all deliberate speed." Although Southern officials seized upon that last phrase to attenuate the process of desegregation, *Brown* marked the beginning of the end of constitutionally sanctioned segregation. In case after case, courts now struck down segregated facilities of all sorts as unconstitutional.

In 1957, the first civil rights act since Reconstruction was passed with President Eisenhower's support, and established the Civil Rights Commission to help formulate a national policy in this area. Still, in the South, *Brown* and similar decisions faced massive resistance. Ninety-six Southern Congressmen signed a declaration urging opposition to integration "by any lawful means." A confrontation of constitutional proportions grew out of Arkansas Governor Orval Faubus's posting of National Guard troops before Central High School in Little Rock to defy a court order that nine black students be admitted. After three weeks of violence, President Eisenhower was forced to dispatch federal troops to Little Rock to escort the black students to school.

The continuing tensions led the school board to petition successfully for a thirty-month delay in the court-ordered desegregation program until "tempers had cooled." The appeal against that delay quickly reached the Supreme Court where the Arkansas ploy was viewed as a direct defiance of the judicial process. In an historic first, all nine Justices signed the opinion of the Court and were treated as equal authors in *Cooper* v. *Aaron* (1958). The Court declared "the federal judiciary is supreme in the exposition of the law of the Constitution, and that principle has ever since been respected by this Court and the Country as a permanent and indispensable feature of our constitutional system." It went on to declare that *Brown* "can neither be nullified openly and directly by state legislators or state executive or judicial officers, nor nullified indirectly by them through evasive schemes."

By then, a broad-based civil rights movement had developed, taking the quest for equality as a "promissory note that had become due," in the words of the Reverend Martin Luther King, Jr. President John F. Kennedy appeared to enlist in the movement by putting the power of the White House behind it. Federal protection was given to young people, known as "freedom riders," who traveled the South integrating lunch

Students of Central High School in Little Rock, Arkansas are shown on the wall and along the stairway leading to the entrance, as they watched federal troops escort eight of the nine black students attending the school, into the building on October 3, 1957. UPI/Bettmann Newsphotos

The Warren Court. 1957–1958. Standing, from left: Associate Justices William J. Brennan, Jr., Tom C. Clark, John M. Harlan, Charles E. Whittaker. Seated, from left: Associate Justices William O. Douglas, Hugo L. Black, Chief Justice Earl Warren, Associate Justices Felix Frankfurter, Harold H. Burton. Collection of the Supreme Court of the United States, Washington, D.C.

counters and other forms of public accommodation, beginning in 1961. Justice Department officials forced Governor George Wallace out of the doorway of the University of Alabama so that black students could enter. By executive order, racial discrimination was prohibited in federally subsidized housing. President Kennedy also appeared on television to support the cause, saying it is "as old as the Scriptures and is as clear as the Constitution."

In the meantime, Dr. King quickly became the leader of the civil rights movement. His "I Have a Dream" speech, celebrating the 100th anniversary of the Emancipation Proclamation, and delivered from the steps of the Lincoln Memorial in Washington, D.C. on August 28, 1963, drew more than 200,000 supporters of all races. It was the high-water mark of the cause that had become known as "The Movement" and helped to secure passage in 1964 of the nation's most important Civil Rights Act, as much a memorial to the efforts of the recently assassinated young president, John F. Kennedy, as to the ongoing civil rights struggle. The same credits are due for ratification in 1964 of the Twentieth Amendment, ending the use of poll taxes to discourage blacks from voting.

Lyndon B. Johnson maintained the momentum John F. Kennedy had initiated. President Johnson declared war on poverty and pushed through a 1965 Voting Rights Act, effectively implementing the Fifteenth Amendment nearly a century after it had been ratified. Fair housing legislation and vigorous enforcement further exemplified Lyndon Johnson's efforts. At Howard University in 1965, he described the challenge that still lay ahead: "You do not take a person who for years has been hobbled by chains and liberate him, bring him up to the starting line of a race and then say, 'you are free to compete with the others,' and still justly believe that you have been completely fair. . . . We seek not just freedom but opportunity. We seek not just legal equity but human ability, not just equality as a right and a theory but equality as a fact and equality as a result."

The Supreme Court also provided encouragement to the movement. In *Heart of Atlanta Motel, Inc.* v. *United States* (1964), Justice Tom C. Clark found that Congress had the power to prohibit discrimination by commercial enterprises engaged in interstate commerce—the basis of the 1964 Civil Rights Act. The most interesting aspect of this opinion upholding the Act's constitutionality came from its resting upon the Constitution's grant of the commerce power, not upon the Fourteenth Amendment.

The activism of the civil rights movement also spawned a resurgent women's movement that won initial congressional

President John F. Kennedy is shown here with Roy Wilkins, NAACP, A. Philip Randolph, a Vice-President of the AFL-CIO, Reverend Martin Luther King, Jr., Southern Christian Leadership Conference, John Lewis, Chairman of the Student Nonviolent Committee, Matthew Ahmann, Executive Director of the National Catholic Conference for Interracial Justice, Dr. Eugene Carson Blake, Vice-Chairman of the Commission on Race Relations for the National Council of Churches, Rabbi Joachim Prinz, Chairman of the American Jewish Congress, and Walter Reuther, President of the United Auto Workers. 1961. UPI/Bettmann Newsphotos

Professor John R. Salter and two other sit-ins shown at a downtown Jackson, Mississippi lunch counter covered with mustard, catsup, and sugar sprayed on them by a crowd of white teenagers in 1963. Although beaten several times on the back and head by an unidentified white man, Professor Salter remained at the counter. UPI/Bettmann Newsphotos

One of the highlights of 1963 was the Civil Rights March on the capital. The huge crowds that poured into Washington, D.C. from all over the country filled the area in front of the Lincoln Memorial and around the Washington Monument Reflection Pool for the ceremonies. This view was taken from the top of the Lincoln Memorial. August 28, 1963. AP/Wide World Photos

Governor George Wallace of Alabama refusing Nicholas Katzenbach of the Justice Department permission to enter the University of Alabama to enroll two black students. June 12, 1963. UPI/Bettmann Newsphotos

President Lyndon B. Johnson is shown at a meeting with Roy Wilkins, Executive Director of the NAACP, James Farmer, National Director of CORE, Reverend Martin Luther King, Jr., Head of the Southern Christian Leadership Conference, and Whitney Young of the Urban League. The subject under discussion was the President's "War on Poverty." January 18, 1964. UPI/Bettmann Newsphotos approval—if not final ratification—of a constitutional amendment guaranteeing equal rights for women. The Equal Rights Amendment (ERA) was actually nothing new; it had been drafted in 1923 by Alice Paul and introduced in Congress each year until 1972, when it finally passed both houses. It failed, however, to gain ratification by the requisite thirty-eight states to become part of the Constitution—although thirteen states added equal rights amendments to their constitutions.

Women were long ignored by the law. Even before American independence had been won, Abigail Adams urged her husband, John, to "remember the ladies" in the new laws that would be necessary after nationhood had been achieved. Nevertheless, Adams and the other leaders did not remember. Until 1840, women in Massachusetts, for example, were forbidden to manage money matters. The law was so stringent that women's sewing clubs were required to have a man responsible for their treasuries. Upon marriage, women surrendered many of the rights they had enjoyed while single, and became the property of their husbands.

Justice Tom C. Clark. 1965. AP/Wide World Photos

The seeds for women's suffrage were planted at a convention dominated by Elizabeth Cady Stanton and Lucretia Mott, as well as by black abolitionist Frederick Douglass, in upstate New York in July 1848. Three hundred men and women attended the Seneca Falls Convention and resolved that women should have the right to vote. Earlier, a brief experiment with voting for women had been tried in New Jersey, but abandoned for lack of participation by women. Upon its admission to the Union in 1890, Wyoming, followed quickly by Colorado, granted women the right to vote. Led by Elizabeth Cady Stanton and Susan B. Anthony, the National Woman Suffrage Association pressed for the vote, winning referendums in Washington (1910), California (1911), Oregon, Arizona, and Kansas (1912), as well as Nevada and Montana (1914). Neither woman, however, lived to see the Nineteenth Amendment, guaranteeing women the right to vote, become part of the Constitution in 1920.

Portrait of Mrs. John Adams by Gilbert Stuart. 1815. National Gallery of Art, Washington, D.C. Gift of Mrs. Robert Homans

Many women had also joined the abolitionist movement in the early nineteenth century. The fight against slavery whetted their appetites for recognition of their own rights. Initially, however, widespread paternal attitudes prevented much progress in this area. Myra Bradwell, a successful Chicago legal publisher, decided to become a lawyer shortly after the Civil War. She passed the Illinois bar examination in 1869, but was denied admission to the bar because of her sex and her status as a married woman. She was not accorded any satisfaction by the Supreme Court in 1873; Justice Bradley wrote: "Man is, or should be, woman's protector and defender. The natural and

Justice Joseph P. Bradley. Collection of the Supreme Court of the United States, Washington, D.C.

proper timidity and delicacy which belongs to the female sex evidently unfits it for many of the occupations of civil life."

The paternalistic attitude of the Court continued to linger—as late as 1961, it still commanded a majority of the Court. Gwendolyn Hoyt was convicted of the second-degree murder of her husband. She appealed, claiming that the exclusion of women from juries in Florida prejudiced her case. Her argument was characterized as claiming that women would have understood what she had done. In *Hoyt* v. *Florida* (1961), the Supreme Court affirmed her conviction. Justice John Harlan, grandson of the *Plessy* dissenter, wrote that "woman is still regarded as the center of home and family life," and she should be protected from the unseemly atmosphere of a criminal trial. It was not until 1975 that the Court reversed this decision and required states to include women on the jury rolls.

The women's movement gradually began to change attitudes, and the Supreme Court decisions began to reflect the new social reality. In 1971, *Reed* v. *Reed* struck down, on the basis of the Fourteenth Amendment's equal protection guarantee, an Idaho law that gave preference to a male over a female parent as administrator of a deceased child's estate. In *Frontiero* v. *Richardson* (1973), a female air force officer had applied for the standard housing and medical benefits afforded other married couples in the air force, but was denied them for her husband because he was not dependent upon her for his support. Male applicants with working wives, however, were

Although Justice Bradley felt that, "The natural and proper timidity and delicacy which belongs to the female sex evidently unfits it for many of the occupations of civil life," the reality of the situation was somewhat different, as shown in these photos.

The Waiting-Room in the building of the Working Woman's Protective Union. 1881. The New-York Historical Society

Young girls at work in a textile mill. Nineteenth-century. Photo by Brown Brothers, Sterling, Pennsylvania

Woman bootmaker. Nineteenth-century. Library of Congress, Washington, D.C.

Young female workers in Pittsburgh. 1908. Division of Archives and Manuscripts. Pennsylvania Historical and Museum Commission, Harrisburg

Female medical helicopter mechanic at Fort Stewart, Georgia. April 18, 1980. United States Army Photograph

Justice William J. Brennan, Jr. UPI/ Bettmann Newsphotos

Chief Justice Warren E. Burger. UPI/ Bettmann Newsphotos

routinely granted these benefits. The Court, with Justice William J. Brennan, Jr. writing a plurality opinion, found the rule discriminatory and one that violated the equal protection guarantee.

If Justice Brennan's opinion had commanded one more vote, an amendment to the Constitution would not have been necessary, because a majority of the Court would have elevated questions of women's rights to the same suspect category as race had received after *Korematsu*. In deciding equal protection questions, the Supreme Court uses two basic classifications: suspect and not suspect. Race and national origin are suspect classes and discrimination on the basis of either is considered unconstitutional unless very compelling evidence is produced to show that the differential treatment is necessary for society's greater good. It is virtually impossible for a classification to survive this level of analysis. Differential treatment of non-suspect classes such as sex can be upheld if there is a "rational basis" for the classification.

While this has led to many difficulties of application, the complexity of equal protection analysis palls when compared to the difficulties of formulating suitable remedies for discrimination. Busing to end racial segregation in the schools, for example, has caused federal judges to become involved in the design of attendance zones and busing routes. Busing remains a highly charged emotional issue. During his presidency, Richard Nixon asked the Justice Department to draft a constitutional amendment that would have prohibited busing as a remedy to correct school segregation.

To avoid busing, some groups have proposed that children ought to be able to attend neighborhood schools. The Supreme Court rejected this notion in *Swann* v. *Charlotte-Mecklenburg Board of Education* (1971). In the Court's opinion, Chief Justice Warren Burger was emphatic that the neighborhood-school concept was sound, all things being equal, but "all things are not equal in a system that has been deliberately constructed and maintained to enforce racial segregation," particularly where it "may fail to counteract the continuing effects of past school segregation resulting from discriminatory location of school sites or distortion of school size."

Still, there are limits to what the courts can do. After finding that the Detroit school system was becoming a black school system, a federal court issued a desegregation plan that included fifty-three Detroit suburbs. The Supreme Court, in *Milliken* v. *Bradley* (1974), found that the lower court had exceeded its power. "Before the boundaries of separate and autonomous school districts may be set aside by consolidating the separate units for remedial purposes or by imposing a cross-

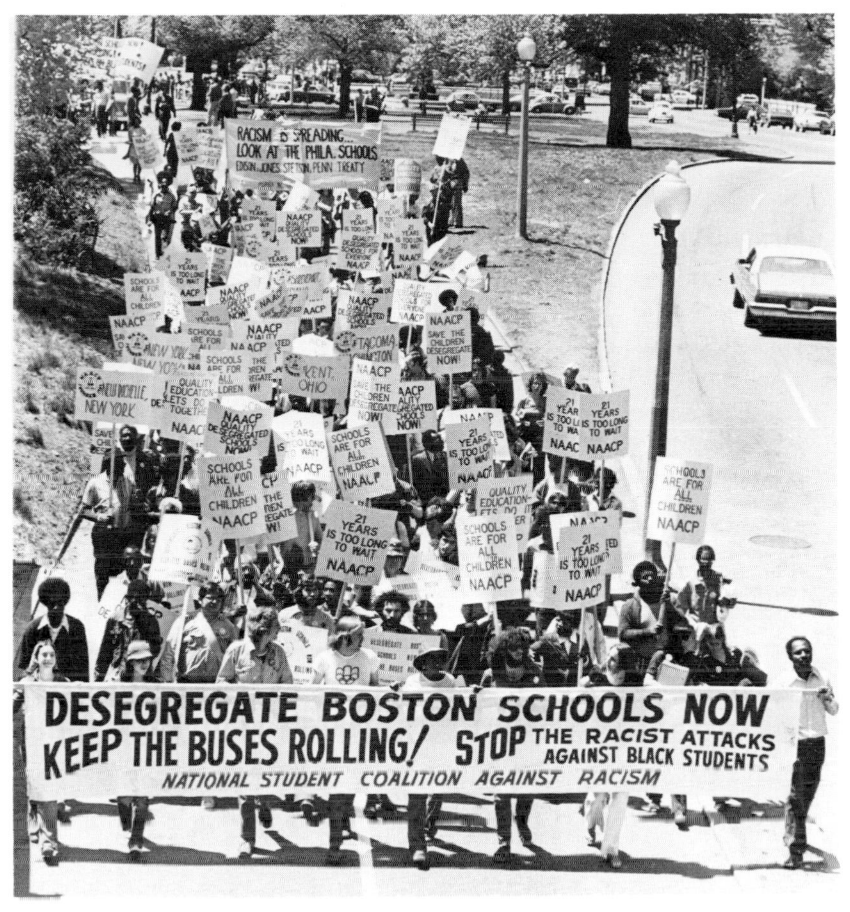

A "National March on Boston," sponsored by the NAACP was held on May 17, 1975 to commemorate the twenty-first anniversary of the United States Supreme Court's decision banning segregated schools, and to support busing to end racial segregation in the schools. UPI/Bettmann Newsphotos

About 2,000 Louisville area opponents of racial busing staged a march from the Ellipse (in back of the White House, top center) to the United States Capitol for a rally. The demonstrators, most of them members of labor unions, came to Washington, D.C. despite the absence of Congress, and a strong disavowal of their cause from the nation's top union leader, AFL-CIO President George Meany. October 25, 1975. UPI/Bettmann Newsphotos

Chief Justice Warren E. Burger and Associate Justice Sandra Day O'Connor. Photo by Timothy A. Murphy. Photo Copyright, 1981, *U.S. News & World Report*

Allan Bakke, right, receiving his degree in medicine from Executive Vice Chancellor Elmer Learn of the University of California Medical School during graduation ceremonies in Davis. 1982. AP/Wide World Photos

district remedy," wrote Chief Justice Burger, "it must first be shown that there has been a constitutional violation within one district that produces a significant segregative effect in another district."

While busing has become the major civil rights issue in the schools, affirmative action programs provide similar difficulties for the courts, although this time in both education and employment. Affirmative action programs are designed to provide women and minorities with opportunities in education and employment that have previously been denied them. This would seem a sufficiently worthy goal to ensure universal approval. But when classroom seats or job openings are limited, someone has to be excluded. The preferential treatment given to women or minorities, some say, constitutes reverse discrimination against members of the majority group. The Supreme Court has struggled with this issue.

It came before the Court when Allan Bakke was denied admission to a California medical school. A special admissions program at the school reserved a number of seats in the class for minority or disadvantaged students. Bakke claimed his exclusion was a direct result of this minority quota. A badly divided Court issued a confusing ruling in *Regents of the University of California* v. *Bakke* (1978). Bakke won his case and was admitted to the school. The Court's plurality found strict racial preferences a violation of the Civil Rights Act—but permitted schools to consider race as one of a number of factors in evaluating applications.

In 1980, the Court upheld the constitutionality of a federal requirement that ten percent of federal public works contracts be set aside for minority-owned businesses in *Fullilove* v. *Klutznik*. Voluntary affirmative action plans, adopted by employers or bargained for by unions, were sanctioned in *United Steel Workers of America* v. *Weber* (1979) to remedy past segregative traditions.

Still, the issues remain vexing. Wendy Wygant and a group of teachers challenged their layoffs by a local school board because preferential treatment had been extended to some minority teachers. A collective bargaining agreement between the board and the teachers' union provided protection against layoffs to teachers with the most seniority, but also stated that "at no time will there be a greater percentage of minority personnel laid off than the current percentage of minority personnel employed at the time of the layoff." Minority teachers had brought a successful lawsuit against the school board in state court earlier to enforce the provision during a prior layoff. Wygant and her colleagues complained that they had greater seniority than the minority teachers who were still on the payroll.

The Burger Court. 1981–1986. Standing, from left: Associate Justices John Paul Stevens, Louis Franklin Powell, Jr., William Hubbs Rehnquist, Sandra Day O'Connor. Seated, from left: Associate Justices Thurgood Marshall, William Joseph Brennan, Jr., Chief Justice Warren E. Burger, Associate Justices Byron Raymond White, Harry A. Blackmun. Photograph by the *National Geographic*. Collection of the Supreme Court of the United States, Washington, D.C.

A plurality of the Supreme Court found that the policy violated the Fourteenth Amendment in *Wygant* v. *Jackson Board of Education* (1986). Justice Lewis F. Powell, Jr. wrote: "This Court never has held that societal discrimination alone is sufficient to justify a racial classification. Rather, the Court has insisted upon some showing of prior discrimination by the governmental unit involved before allowing limited use of racial classifications in order to remedy such discrimination." The opinion also found it improper to try to remedy the continuing effects of past discrimination in this manner when other less intrusive means, such as the adoption of hiring goals, were available.

Questions of affirmative action, as well as of race and sex discrimination, will not cease to arise, and the issues will continue to appear in various guises before the courts. It is their province to attempt to steer a wise course through the thickets ahead. In 1948, commenting upon an entirely different issue, Justice Douglas observed that "there are few areas of the law in black and white. The greys are dominant and even among them the shades are innumerable. For the eternal problem of the law is one of making accommodations between conflicting

As Justice Douglas observed: ". . . the eternal problem of the law is one of making accommodations between conflicting interests." The shift in expectations as a result of legal accommodations reached between labor and management is obvious here in the changing stance of labor, first in the early 1900s, and then in 1937.

Breaker Boys at a Pennsylvania coal mine. c. 1900. Library of Congress, Washington, D.C.

United Auto Workers organizers Robert Kanter, Walter Reuther, Richard Frankensteen, and J.J. Kennedy prepare to greet members of the Ford Motor Company Service Department at the Ford Rouge plant in Dearborn, Michigan. May 26, 1937. The Archives of Labor and Urban Affairs, Wayne State University

Justice Felix Frankfurter. UPI/ Bettmann Newsphotos

interests. This is why most legal problems end as questions of degree."

Still, the courts are loathe to become involved in issues that have not matured as legal questions. "History teaches that the independence of the judiciary," Justice Felix Frankfurter admonished, "is jeopardized when courts become embroiled in the passions of the day and assume primary responsibility in choosing between competing political, economic and social pressures."

Ultimately, it will be up to the American people to resolve the difficult issues that discrimination will continue to present, not just in the areas of race and sex, but for people discriminated against because of age, handicapped conditions, poverty, or their immigration status. In the *Civil Rights Cases* (1883), Justice Bradley offered a premature but noteworthy hope: "When a man has emerged from slavery, and by the aid of beneficent legislation has shaken off the inseparable concomitants of that state, there must be some stage in the progress of his elevation when he takes the rank of a mere citizen, and ceases to be the special favorite of the laws, and when his rights as a citizen, or a man, are to be protected in the ordinary modes by which other men's rights are protected."

That day, for both men and women, will not dawn solely as a result of the power wielded by the courts in accordance with their enforcement of constitutional guarantees. At best, the courts may be able to prevent us from slipping backward, but even that effort places great strain upon the institution of the judiciary and its capacities. True equality before the law, in fact as well as in statute, can be achieved only in an atmosphere of good will, and by the united efforts of "We the People."

Chief Justice Earl Warren, President Richard M. Nixon, and Chief Justice Warren E. Burger on the steps of the Supreme Court building after Chief Justice Burger had been sworn in as the fifteenth Chief Justice of the United States. June 1969. UPI/ Bettmann Newsphotos

Associate Justice Antonin Scalia, Chief Justice Warren E. Burger, and Chief Justice William H. Rehnquist in front of the Supreme Court building after Justice Scalia and Chief Justice Rehnquist had been sworn in. September 1986. Jose R. Lopez/*The New York Times*

The members of the Supreme Court of the United States from 1789 to 1925, and the Supreme Court Chamber in the Capitol. Collection of the Supreme Court of the United States, Washington, D.C.

The 1889 Oklahoma land rush began at noon on April 22. Here, ready for business, a frontier lawyer has set up his office. Western History Collections, University of Oklahoma Library

Whether in formal attire or in business suits, whether in the shadow of Cass Gilbert's marble pillars or at a respectful distance, whether somber-natured or cheerful and gregarious—or even, by necessity, conducting legal affairs outdoors with few frills and no overhead—the members of the judiciary have continually been called upon by the citizenry to mediate, to harmonize, to balance those "conflicting interests" of which Justice Douglas spoke. And always, they must strive against the kind of impatience reflected in the jingle pinned to the body of a man hanged by Vigilantes in Casper, Wyoming in 1902:

Process of law is a little slow
So this is the road you'll have to go.
Murderers and thieves, Beware!
PEOPLE'S VERDICT.

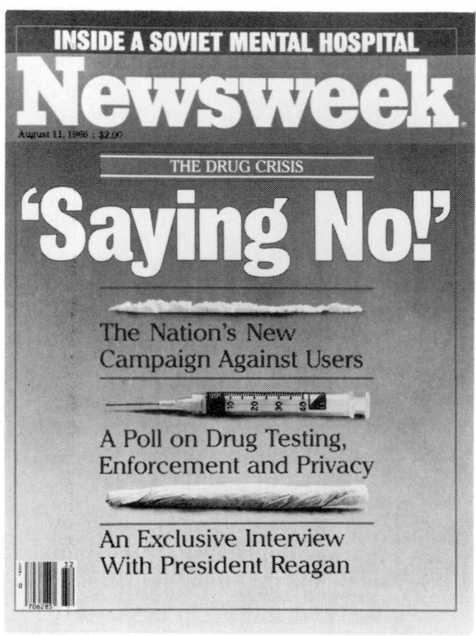

INSIDE A SOVIET MENTAL HOSPITAL
Newsweek
THE DRUG CRISIS
'Saying No!'
The Nation's New
Campaign Against Users
A Poll on Drug Testing,
Enforcement and Privacy
An Exclusive Interview
With President Reagan

Cover of *Newsweek* Magazine highlighting "The Drug Crisis." August 11, 1986. Copyright 1986, by Newsweek, Inc. All rights reserved. Reprinted by permission.

PART III

Rights of the Accused

Crime is one of the most vexing of contemporary problems. An understandable fear of violence and a growing victim's rights movement have brought heightened attention to the results of crime, and the shattered lives it leaves in its wake.

Often, the public's frustration takes the form of complaints about coddling criminals. They have *too many* rights, some say. The point is made that some criminals have escaped punishment because of "legal technicalities," and the courts have been accused of handcuffing the police and preventing them from doing their job. In various forums, Attorney General Edwin Meese III has repeated his claim that the constitutionally based protections afforded the accused help only the guilty, while distorting the criminal justice system. Those on the other side of the debate adhere strictly to the belief that less vigilant protection of the rights of criminal suspects would eventually lead to infringements of *everyone's* rights.

Currently, the criminal issue that appears to top the crime charts in terms of public awareness and alarm is the use of illegal narcotics. The introduction of a cheap form of cocaine, known as crack, the narcotics-related deaths of two prominent athletes, and growing evidence of the widespread recreational use of drugs by young, upper-income men and women have catapulted the issue onto the covers of major magazines—a reliable barometer of public concern. People want something done about the problem, and many politicians have added their voices to the public outcry. The difficult task, however, is to devise effective solutions that will meet constitutional requirements. An old saying—what goes around, comes around—pinpoints the dilemma that is at the very heart of these vital constitutional guarantees.

President Reagan's response to the narcotics problem in 1986 included a drug-test proposal that would affect nearly half the civilian federal work force—some 1.1 million employees. These people are not specifically suspected of narcotics use, but are considered to hold "sensitive" positions in the national defense, law enforcement, or public health and safety sectors, or are presidential appointees. Police and fire departments have followed the president's lead in attempting to institute drug tests that are being resisted by those public servants affected, who feel they have done nothing to deserve this generalized suspicion. Ironically, in suing to have the tests declared unconstitutional, police officers are raising precisely the same issue—the need for individualized suspicion—that has evoked public impatience with the constitutional "technicalities" found in the Fourth Amendment to the Constitution.

The Fourth Amendment protects people, their houses, their papers, and their property against unreasonable searches and seizures by the government. This protection usually arises when the police are seeking evidence of a crime, but the guarantee also applies to the process of arresting a criminal suspect. Before the police can begin a search of private property, the Constitution compels them to obtain a search warrant, even, for example, when police want to look inside a locked trunk that they took into custody during the course of an arrest.

The reason for requiring a warrant was explained by Justice William O. Douglas as a protection against the "casual arrogance of those who have the untrammelled power to invade one's home and to seize one's person." The warrant requirements recognize the privacy rights of those suspected, balancing them against the needs of those authorities actively engaged in ferreting out crime. It seeks to inject an orderly procedure for investigation and arrest into the criminal justice system. As a result, law enforcement officials must seek authorization from a presumably detached and neutral magistrate, independent of both the police and prosecution.

A neutral judgment is necessary. The presumption of innocence applicable in the courtroom cannot realistically be observed by police officers who are not empowered to judge, but rather must capture a suspect they have reason to believe is

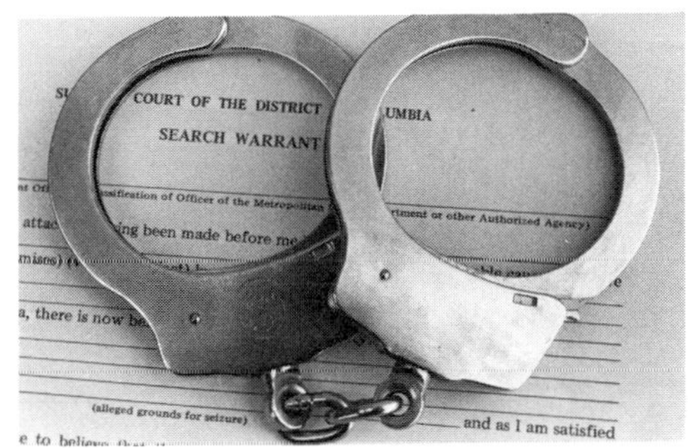

Before the police can engage in a search of private property, the Fourth Amendment requires that a search warrant be issued by a judicial officer upon a showing that probable cause exists that evidence of a crime will be found. Photo: Paul Conklin

Justice William O. D
Collection of
the United S

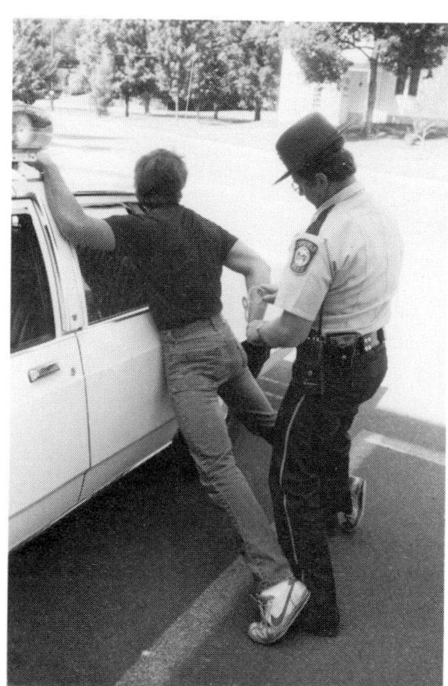

The police have greater authority to "stop and frisk" an individual acting suspiciously in the open than they have to search a person's home. Photo: Paul Conklin (Monkmeyer Photos)

guilty of a crime. Without the warrant procedure, it is possible to imagine corners being cut ever more closely until disregard of proper procedures by police could become the norm, rather than the exception.

Using this rationale, Judge H. Lee Sarokin struck down a Plainfield, New Jersey drug-testing plan that applied to police and firefighters. On May 26, 1986 at seven o'clock in the morning, city officials awakened firefighters at the firehouse for a surprise urine test. Those who refused to take the test were told they would face immediate dismissal. Sixteen men were fired after their test results were declared positive.

"If we choose to violate the rights of the innocent in order to discover the guilty," wrote Judge Sarokin in striking down the Plainfield plan, "then we will have transformed our country into a police state. . . . In order to win the war against drugs, we must not sacrifice the life of the Constitution in the battle."

In another case, Judge Robert F. Collins in New Orleans declared that urine tests of federal employees conducted before witnesses are "a gross invasion of privacy so detracting from human dignity it shocks the conscience and offends this court's sense of justice." While both drug-test decisions will be appealed, these judges agreed that the Fourth Amendment requires individualized suspicion sufficient to support a warrant before an agent of the government can invade a person's privacy in this manner. The dangers of leaving searches for illegal activity to the unfettered discretion of the authorities can result in the very horror stories that specific provisions in the Constitution were intended to prevent.

That is what happened on November 26, 1965, when six federal narcotics agents entered the home of Webster Bivens in New York, manacled him in front of his wife and children, threatened to arrest his family if they interfered, made a thorough search of his apartment, and arrested him on drug charges. He was then interrogated at the agents' office, fingerprinted, photographed, booked, and subjected to a strip search. All of this was done without a search or an arrest warrant. The Commissioner who heads the Federal Bureau of Narcotics eventually dismissed the complaint against Bivens, who then sued for the trespass and humiliation caused him. In a 1971 decision—six years after the break-in by federal agents—the United States Supreme Court held that Bivens had a right to sue, and allowed him to press his action for $90,000 in damages against the Bureau.

Constitutional mandates compel the police and the courts to pay careful attention to the warrant provision. The Fourth Amendment states that a search warrant is issued only upon a showing of "probable cause, supported by Oath or affirmation

The use of metal detectors has become widespread, as shown here with penitentiary inmates returning from a work detail. But the use of metal detectors at airports caused some individuals to complain that their right to privacy was infringed. The courts, however, have found such security searches reasonable. Photo: Mimi Forsyth (Monkmeyer Photos)

. . . " that evidence of criminality is likely to be found. Without any of the ambiguity in other provisions of the Constitution, this amendment requires that the warrant particularly describe ". . . the place to be searched, and the persons or things to be seized." Despite the specificity of that requirement, courts have been forced repeatedly to examine the issue of what constitutes a reasonable search or seizure, and which specific actions could transform an otherwise reasonable search into an unconstitutional one. The test used by the courts relies upon the individual facts and circumstances of each case, and involves a careful weighing of society's interest in crime prevention and detection against an individual's right to privacy.

The courts recognize several common-sense exceptions to the warrant requirement. An officer making an arrest, for example, has the authority to search for weapons in the immediate area where the arrest is made, in order to protect himself, or to seize evidence likely to be destroyed during the time it would take to secure a warrant. Police are permitted to peer into a motor vehicle and discover anything open to view. An expanded search of a car may take place when the driver is taken into custody. Also, when a suspect runs into a building to evade capture, the police are in "hot pursuit" and do not need a warrant to follow him into the building.

When airports began using metal detectors and searching passengers to prevent skyjackings, many people complained,

Justice Potter Stewart. Collection of the Supreme Court of the United States, Washington, D.C.

but the courts found the searches reasonable. With the growing danger of terrorism, it is possible that a future court's finding concerning "reasonableness" may differ from that which the courts would consider an affront to the Fourth Amendment today. This changing standard of reasonableness could conceivably apply in the context of drug testing as well, whether in the appeals that are now pending, or in future cases. This may seem to make it difficult to arrive at a clear understanding of the Fourth Amendment's requirements, but it is also a necessary part of our constitutional system. The general principles enunciated in the Constitution and elaborated upon by the courts require considered application. If the courts did not weigh the different factors involved in a particular case and the context within which they arose, the law would most certainly appear to be the ass that Charles Dickens's Mr. Bumble declared it to be.

Today, the reasonableness of a search is linked to the normal "expectation of privacy" that each individual is considered to enjoy. A police officer hardly has to turn away to avoid seeing criminal activity taking place in clear view. Nor is he acting improperly when he uses evidence that has been shown to others who have no interest in keeping it private. The police can also search a premise with the consent of the owner or someone else in authority, such as a spouse, friend, business partner, employee, or roommate.

When television police dramas show a transmitter attached to the bottom of a suspect's car in order to track it, the fictional police are engaged in a legal search since there can be no expectation of privacy in a vehicle being driven on the open road. However, once such a vehicle pulls into a private garage, a warrant would be necessary to continue tracking the car by the beeper device.

The modern emphasis upon a person's expectation of privacy stems from a 1967 Supreme Court decision, *Katz* v. *United States*. Charles Katz was convicted of transmitting wagering information by telephone across state lines in violation of federal law. At his trial, the government used recordings of Katz's public telephone conversations, obtained by attaching an electronic listening and recording device to the booth. Katz claimed the evidence was of illegal origin and sought to have it excluded from the trial. The Supreme Court found that the means of gathering the evidence violated the Fourth Amendment.

"For the Fourth Amendment protects people, not places," Justice Potter Stewart wrote. "What a person knowingly exposes to the public, even in his own home or office, is not a subject of Fourth Amendment protection. . . . But what he seeks to preserve as private, even in an area accessible to the public, may be constitutionally protected."

The Court rejected the claim of the government that because the calls were made from a glass-enclosed telephone booth Katz could not have expected that his conversations would remain private. Justice Stewart found ". . . what he sought to exclude when he entered the booth was not the intruding eye—it was the uninvited ear. He did not shed his right to do so simply because he made his calls from a place where he might be seen. . . . One who occupies [a telephone booth], shuts the door behind him, and pays the toll that permits him to place a call is surely entitled to assume that the words he utters into the mouthpiece will not be broadcast to the world. To read the Constitution more narrowly is to ignore the vital role that the public telephone has come to play in private communication."

The Court also found that the agents would most likely have been able to secure a warrant to authorize the telephone tap, since they had established a strong probability that Katz was using the telephone for unlawful purposes, and had found that he used it for about three minutes at the same time each morning.

The Fourth Amendment's privacy protection traces its lineage back to the American colonial experience with "general warrants." General warrants gave British officers carte blanche to search homes and arrest undesirables. Writs of assistance were a form of general warrant that authorized an unspecified search for contraband. Under these warrants, innocent people were frequently rounded up, arrested, and their belongings confiscated. The practice was often used by revenue officers as an early form of surprise tax audit to see whether people were withholding tribute due the king. General warrants were an invention of the notorious Star Chamber, the judicial arm of the politically powerful King's Council. It used the device to sweep away all opposition.

General warrants were a major source of resentment in the colonies. Americans took a position outlined by Sir William Blackstone in his legal commentaries: a general warrant "to apprehend all persons suspected, without naming or particularly describing any person . . . is illegal and void for its uncertainty." In a list of grievances drawn up at a town meeting, Bostonians included one that stated, "our houses and even our bed chambers are exposed to be ransacked, our boxes, chests, and trunks broke open, ravaged and plundered by wretches, whom no prudent man would venture to employ even as menial servants." John Adams believed the seed for the American revolt was planted in that meeting. "Then and there," he said, "the

The seeds of the English tradition of common law—a formidable structure of fair rules, rights, and obligations protecting liberty from kingly caprice—had taken root in the colonies and would bear fruit in the American Revolution. The influence of the English parliamentary structure, moreover, would become evident in the formation of the new government of the United States of America.

The House of Commons. 1640. Copyright British Museum

Both Houses of Parliament (upper level: House of Lords; lower level: House of Commons) with Charles I presiding. 1641. Copyright British Museum

The Trial of Charles I. January 1649. Copyright British Museum

child Independence was born."

In the 1776 Virginia Declaration of Rights, the state's first constitution, George Mason wrote that general warrants "are grievous and oppressive, and ought not be granted."

Many revolutionary leaders believed that freedom from unwarranted searches and seizures was a natural right of mankind. It didn't require constitutional protection, for it existed with or without that acknowledgment. When, in 1787, the home of Benjamin Frisbie was searched for stolen pork, Connecticut's Superior Court ruled (without benefit of the federal Constitution—only then being written—and without any bill of rights or any comparable state constitutional protection) that the search and Frisbie's arrest had been under a general warrant and thus "clearly illegal."

When the Fourth Amendment was added to the Constitution as an expression of what was generally considered to be an existing right, it most clearly realized the ideal expressed some time earlier by William Pitt the Elder, Earl of Chatham:

> The poorest man may in his cottage bid defiance to all the forces of the Crown. It may be frail—its roof may shake—the wind may blow through it—the storm may enter—the rain may enter but the King of England cannot enter—all his forces dare not cross the threshold of the ruined tenement.

For more than a century, the Fourth Amendment was a dormant giant. The federal government did not have many criminal statutes; crime was more of a state matter. Federal law enforcement officials were rarely in a position to violate citizens' rights.

What happens, though, when the government violates these constitutionally guaranteed rights? A lawsuit for monetary damages—limited by the law to compensation for physical injury to person and property—is an inadequate remedy in most instances. The Supreme Court faced this dilemma in *Weeks* v. *United States* (1914). Weeks was arrested without a warrant and eventually charged with the use of the mails to conduct a lottery, a violation of federal law. While he was under arrest, police officers went to his home, located a key to the house through a neighbor, and entered, taking away papers and other belongings. The materials seized were turned over to federal authorities. The United States marshal returned to the Weeks home later that day and seized additional papers, including some personal letters, a leather grip, a tin box, stocks and bonds, and a souvenir newspaper dating back to 1790. No warrants were ever sought for any of this activity. When the defense counsel sought return of the personal papers and prop-

Sir William Blackstone's stand against general warrants, as expressed in his commentaries on the common law, was more readily accepted by the American colonists than by his compatriots. National Portrait Gallery, London

George Mason of Virginia opposed the federal Constitution because it lacked a Bill of Rights. Courtesy Virginia State Library, Richmond

Newport Superior Court. The opinion in a 1914 case established what is now known as the "exclusionary rule," making evidence obtained in violation of the Fourth Amendment to the Constitution inadmissible in criminal proceedings. UPI/Bettmann Newsphotos

erty, the marshal's office returned those irrelevant to the case, but only after being ordered to do so by the court. Weeks challenged his subsequent conviction because of the Fourth Amendment violation.

In reversing the conviction, Justice William Rufus Day wrote for a unanimous Supreme Court:

> If letters and private documents can thus be seized and held and used in evidence against a citizen accused of an offense, the protection of the Fourth Amendment declaring his right to be secure against such searches and seizures is of no value, and, so far as those thus placed are concerned, might as well be stricken from the Constitution.

Justice William Rufus Day. Courtesy Brown Brothers, Sterling, Pennsylvania

The Court held that "[t]he efforts of the courts and their officials to bring the guilty to punishment, praiseworthy as they are, are not to be aided by the sacrifice of those great principles . . . " The result of the decision is that evidence obtained in violation of the Fourth Amendment is inadmissible at trial. By searching for and taking the papers in violation of the warrant provisions, the law enforcement officials violated the law. If the police, in the course of their duties, violate the law, who will arrest them? If prosecutors who want this evidence to obtain a conviction, condone the police misconduct, who will prosecute them? The Court found that the only way to discourage illegal searches and seizures is to deny police and prosecution the use of any ill-gotten goods.

The Court's opinion established what is now known as the exclusionary rule, holding that evidence seized in violation of the Fourth Amendment is inadmissible in a criminal proceeding. The reasons for the exclusionary rule have been variously stated:

1. To prevent the courts from becoming "accomplices in the willful disobedience of a Constitution they are sworn to uphold."
2. "To deter—to compel respect for the constitutional guaranty in the only effectively available way—by removing the incentive to disregard it."
3. To assure "the people—all potential victims of unlawful government conduct—that the government would not profit from its lawless behavior."

The unanimity of the *Weeks* decision, and the logical reasoning behind the application of the exclusionary rule, have not prevented it from becoming the object of considerable public disaffection. In refusing to adopt the rule in New York, then-Judge Benjamin Cardozo (later to become a United States Supreme Court Justice), derogatively described it as, "the criminal is to go free because the constable has blundered." Others have criticized the rule because it can exclude from the trial evidence crucial to a determination of the truth.

Justice Oliver Wendell Holmes, Jr., in a dissent that was later vindicated by *Katz*, answered Cardozo, saying, "for my part I think it a less evil that some criminals should escape than that the government should play an ignoble part. . . . If the existing code does not permit district attorneys to have a hand in such dirty business, it does not permit the judge to allow such iniquities to succeed."

As might be expected, the rhetoric on the issue has often outstripped its actual impact. Certainly, since *Weeks* was decided in 1914, the FBI and other federal law enforcement agencies operating under the restrictions of the exclusionary rule have not exactly been rendered ineffective. In 1985, a *Chicago Tribune* study conducted over thirteen months found fewer than one percent of Chicago cases involving violent crimes were dismissed due to illegally seized evidence. The survey discovered that evidence was suppressed in only one of every 200 violent crimes and one of every 500 property crimes. In many of the cases where evidence was held inadmissible, the defendant was convicted anyway. Drug cases proved the exception, with thirteen percent affected. The 1985 survey nearly mirrored a 1979 study by the General Accounting Office. The GAO found that motions to suppress evidence were successful in only 1.3 percent of the 3,000 federal cases they studied.

In separate opinions, Justices Benjamin Cardozo and Oliver Wendell Holmes, Jr. seemed to debate the wisdom of the exclusionary rule. The debate continues today.

Justice Benjamin Cardozo. Collection of the Supreme Court of the United States, Washington, D.C.

Justice Oliver Wendell Holmes, Jr. Collection of the Supreme Court of the United States, Washington, D.C.

Justice Felix Frankfurter wrote the opinion of the Supreme Court in *Wolf* v. *Colorado* (1949) that found the Fourth Amendment—but not the exclusionary rule—binding upon the states. Collection of the Supreme Court of the United States, Washington, D.C.

Justice Tom C. Clark wrote the decision for the Supreme Court in *Mapp* v. *Ohio* (1961), in which the Court overturned the conviction of Dollree Mapp on obscenity charges. The Court ruled that the evidence against Mapp could not be used in court because it had been obtained through an illegal search. This case changed the methods and procedures of law enforcement. Collection of the Supreme Court of the United States, Washington, D.C.

The exclusionary rule does sometimes result in the dismissal of charges against a notorious criminal suspect. For that reason, its use—and description as a "technicality"—will continue to raise the public's hackles. The courts, implicitly recognizing public perceptions, have proceeded cautiously with the rule's application.

The *Weeks* decision applied only to the papers taken by the United States marshal, not to those taken by the local police because then-existing interpretations held the Fourth Amendment inapplicable to the states. This changed in 1949. "The security of one's privacy," wrote Justice Felix Frankfurter in *Wolf* v. *Colorado*, "against arbitrary intrusion by the police—which is at the core of the Fourth Amendment—is basic to a free society." However, the Court refused to apply the exclusionary rule as well, finding it a "matter of judicial implication." The Court instead allowed the states an adequate opportunity to adopt the *Weeks* approach (Iowa had an exclusionary rule before *Weeks*), or to find another remedy for police misconduct.

At the time *Wolf* was decided, twenty-nine states had rejected the exclusionary rule, eighteen had adopted it, and one had not yet decided. By 1960, twenty-six states had followed *Weeks*, while twenty-four still admitted the evidence. When the Supreme Court faced the issue again in 1961, the Court noted a trend in favor of exclusion.

Dollree Mapp was convicted of possessing obscene materials, but challenged this result on the basis of the Fourth Amendment. On May 23, 1957, three Cleveland police officers had arrived at her second floor apartment in search of a person wanted for questioning in connection with a bombing in front of the home of Don King, who later gained fame as a fight promoter. The person the police were seeking was visiting the apartment below Mapp's. When the police knocked on her door, Mapp telephoned an attorney representing her in a civil matter and, on his advice, refused to admit the police without a search warrant. Three hours later, the officers returned with at least four others. When Mapp did not immediately answer their knock, they broke the door down. She demanded to see their warrant and was shown a piece of paper, which she grabbed and placed in her blouse. The officers recovered the paper after a struggle and handcuffed her for "belligerency." Her lawyer arrived but the police refused to admit him, or to grant him access to his client.

An extensive search was conducted by the officers. The police looked through Mapp's dresser, drawers, closet, suitcases, and finally a trunk found in the basement where they discovered a sex book from Paris and a number of nude

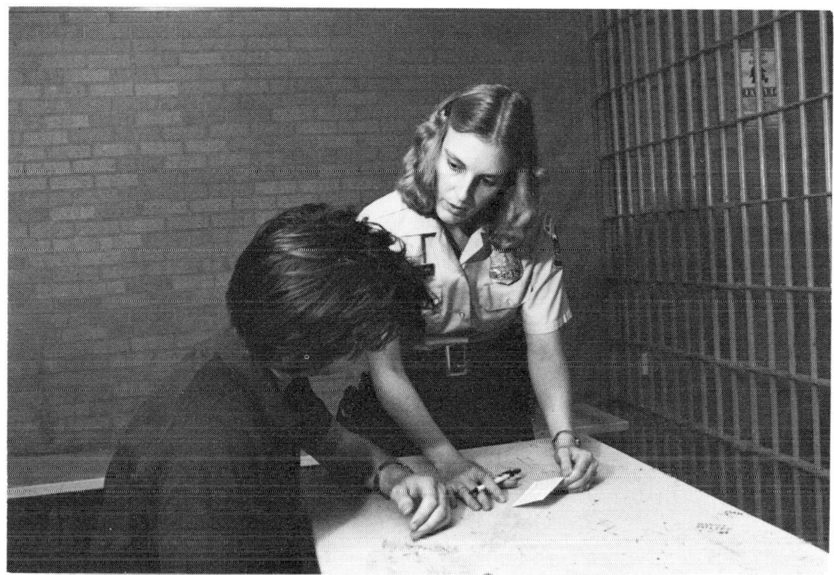

After the *Mapp* decision, police training was adjusted to emphasize the meaning of the Fourth Amendment, and to develop proper procedures for establishing probable cause and obtaining warrants. Photo: Paul Conklin

sketches; these were the obscene materials she was arrested for possessing. At trial, no warrant was produced, leading the Ohio supreme court in reviewing the case to state, "there is, in the record, considerable doubt as to whether there ever was any [warrant]."

In determining that the Fourth Amendment had been egregiously violated and that the exclusionary rule was the only available deterrent to future police violations, the Supreme Court recognized that California had recently adopted the rule after failing in several other attempts at remedies. "Nothing can destroy a government more quickly," wrote Justice Tom Clark for the Court, "than its failure to observe its own laws, or worse, its disregard of the charter of its own existence."

Mapp v. *Ohio* (1961) caused quite a change in law enforcement procedures. One police official in New York City told *The New York Times* after the decision, "We had to reorganize our thinking, frankly. Before this nobody bothered to take out search warrants."

While the *Mapp* case stands for the proposition that evidence obtained illegally cannot be used in court, police and prosecutors have fought to keep evidence before the court when there is a logical reason to justify what might be considered a "technical violation." In 1984, the Supreme Court considered a trio of cases raising this issue and sided with the law enforcement officials. In *United States* v. *Leon*, the Court held that the exclusionary rule does not apply to evidence obtained by officers acting in reasonable ("good faith") reliance upon a search warrant later found to be insufficiently supported by probable cause. To exclude this evidence, the Court reasoned, would not have a deterrent effect.

Another of the 1984 cases, *Nix* v. *Williams*, used the same reasoning to permit the use of evidence obtained by improper means if "the information ultimately or inevitably would have been discovered by lawful means." The third of the cases, *New York* v. *Quarles*, created a "public safety" exception to the requirement that a suspect be read his rights before his statement or any evidence located as a result are admissible as evidence. Police, the Court declared, may question a suspect concerning the whereabouts of a loaded gun posing a safety hazard, before advising him of his rights.

Chief Justice Warren E. Burger wrote the Supreme Court's opinion in *Nix* v. *Williams* (1984), a case involving the Christmas Eve search for a young girl's body. The suspect led police to the body after they appealed to his conscience. Collection of the Supreme Court of the United States, Washington, D.C.

DEFENDANT | LOCATION

SPECIFIC WARNING REGARDING INTERROGATIONS

1. YOU HAVE THE RIGHT TO REMAIN SILENT.
2. ANYTHING YOU SAY CAN AND WILL BE USED AGAINST YOU IN A COURT OF LAW.
3. YOU HAVE THE RIGHT TO TALK TO A LAWYER AND HAVE HIM PRESENT WITH YOU WHILE YOU ARE BEING QUESTIONED.
4. IF YOU CANNOT AFFORD TO HIRE A LAWYER ONE WILL BE APPOINTED TO REPRESENT YOU BEFORE ANY QUESTIONING, IF YOU WISH ONE.

SIGNATURE OF DEFENDANT | DATE

WITNESS | TIME

☐ REFUSED SIGNATURE SAN FRANCISCO POLICE DEPARTMENT PR.9.1.4

Arrest Card used by the San Francisco Police Department to inform suspects of their rights. Bettmann Archive

The Supreme Court has also been asked to define the extent to which school children are protected against searches conducted by school officials. T.L.O., a name used to protect the identity of the accused fourteen-year-old Piscataway, New Jersey high school student, was caught with a friend smoking in the lavatory in violation of school regulations. Both girls were taken to the principal's office. One girl admitted to assistant vice principal Theodore Choplick that she had been smoking, but T.L.O. denied she smoked at all.

Choplick examined T.L.O.'s purse and found a pack of cigarettes, together with rolling papers used to smoke marijuana. A further search of the purse yielded a small amount of marijuana, a pipe, empty plastic bags, a substantial wad of one-dollar bills, a list of students owing T.L.O. money, and two letters implicating her in dealing the drug.

T.L.O.'s parents were notified, and the evidence obtained in the search was turned over to the police. Delinquency charges were brought, and T.L.O. was placed on one year's probation. The case reached the Supreme Court based on whether Choplick's search of T.L.O.'s purse violated the Fourth Amendment.

It has been well-recognized that students do not "shed their constitutional rights . . . at the schoolhouse gate." In *New Jersey* v. *T.L.O.* (1985), the Court determined that the Fourth Amendment does apply to students, and minors do retain an expectation of privacy while at school. Nevertheless, schools also have a legitimate interest in maintaining security and order, as well as in preserving a certain degree of informality in the student-teacher relationship. Warrants, therefore, are inappropriate in a school environment. Justice Byron White wrote for the Court that "the legality of a search of a student should depend simply on the reasonableness, under all the circumstances, of the search." The search of T.L.O.'s purse was reasonable, the Court concluded.

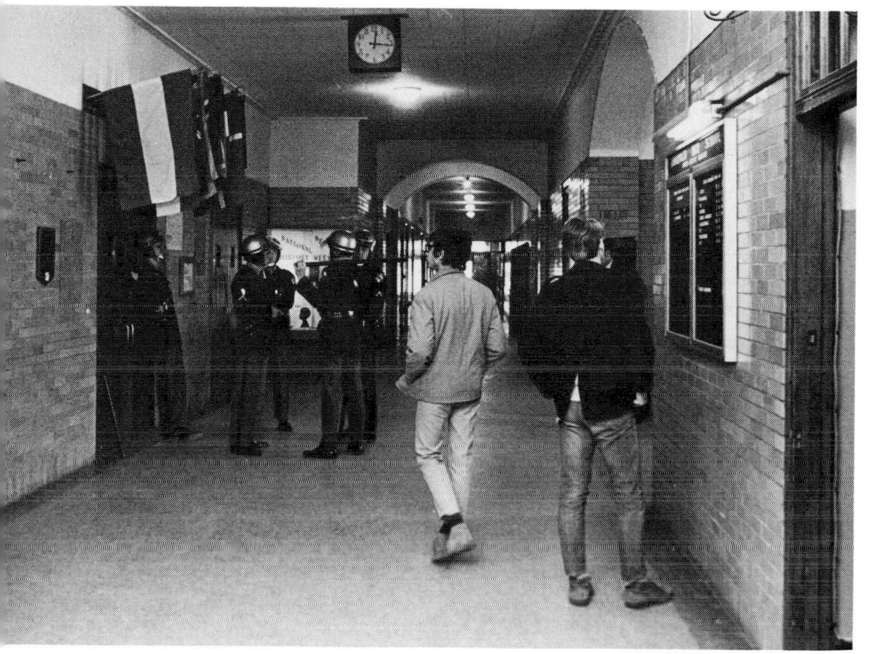

The rights of students, particularly in regard to searches, have been debated before the Supreme Court several times in recent years. While students do not "shed their constitutional rights . . . at the schoolhouse gate," the need to maintain discipline and order can sometimes outweigh a student's interest in personal privacy. UPI/ Bettmann Newsphotos

While much attention is paid to how evidence is obtained, the Fourth Amendment's requirement of probable cause also affects the discretion police officers have to stop and question an individual. Probable cause, necessary for the police to make an arrest, depends on the "factual and practical considerations of everyday life." For this reason, the Court has ruled that police knowledge of a suspect's reputation can be a factor in determining probable cause. The suspicion must be of a particular offense that has been or is being committed; it cannot be a generalized suspicion leading to an arrest for purposes of investigating further. Arrests for vagrancy, based upon the theory that vagrancy and criminal activity go hand-in-hand, are not permitted.

Once a suspect is taken into custody, as everyone who watches television knows, he is read his Miranda rights. Television police dramas have done much to make these warnings a part of the public's knowledge. The warnings effectuate the Fifth Amendment's guarantee that no one "shall be compelled in any criminal case to be a witness against himself." It is this provision that is invoked when someone "takes the Fifth."

Invoking this privilege does not necessarily imply guilt. A desire for privacy, loyalty to friends who may or may not be guilty, or a refusal to be part of an ill-considered prosecution, are all legitimate motivations for standing on Fifth Amendment rights.

Justice Byron R. White wrote the Supreme Court's opinion in *New Jersey* v. *T.L.O.*, upholding the search of a high school student's purse on the ground that "the legality of a search of a student should depend simply on the reasonableness, under all the circumstances, of the search." Collection of the Supreme Court of the United States, Washington, D.C.

In 1947, ten screenwriters, known as the "Hollywood Ten," refused to answer questions about their alleged Communist activities before the House Un-American Activities Committee on the ground that their testimony might incriminate them—that is, they invoked the Fifth Amendment. The "Hollywood Ten," shown here, included Herbert Biberman, Albert Maltz, Lester Cole, Dalton Trumbo, John Howard Lawson, Alvah Bessie, Samuel Ornitz, Ring Lardner, Jr., Edward Dymtryk, and Adrian Scott. The Museum of Modern Art/Film Stills Archive

The Names of the Jury of Life and Death. 1649.
Copyright British Museum

The Great Seal of Massachusetts illustrates the high regard in which the Massachusetts Colony held the rights heralded by the Magna Carta.

Justice Felix Frankfurter explained the basis for this constitutional right in *Watts* v. *Indiana* (1949): "Ours is the accusatorial as opposed to the inquisitorial system. Such has been the characteristic of Anglo-American criminal justice since it freed itself from practices borrowed by the Star Chamber from the Continent. . . . Under our system society carries the burden of proving the charges against the accused not out of his own mouth."

In England, the High Commission Court had been accuser, prosecutor, judge, and jury against those who disagreed with it. It was an ecclesiastical court, as was the Star Chamber, which often used torture to secure confessions. In the early seventeenth century, both fell under the control of the notorious William Laud, Archbishop of Canterbury, who used it to crush opposition to the rule of King Charles I. To assist its work, the Commission required those called before it to take an oath *ex officio*, promising to answer all questions truthfully. The effect was to require the accused to admit their guilt. Those who refused to take the oath were deemed to have confessed, since only the guilty would have anything to hide. Those punished were fined, imprisoned, and sometimes mutilated. William Prynne, a Presbyterian who had attacked the Church of England, had his ears cut off and "SL"—for seditious libeler—branded on his cheeks.

The right against self incrimination later established in England was easily transported to the American colonies, together with the common-law tradition. It underwent a period of further development, though. In the Massachusetts Body of Liberties of 1641, an early colonial constitution, Article 45 stated:

> No man shall be forced by Torture to confesse any Crime against himselfe nor any other unlesse it be in some Capitall case where he is first fullie convicted by cleare and suffitient evidence to be guilty . . . [then to discover his confederates] he may be tortured, yet not with such Tortures as be Barbarous and inhumane.

Many early cases arose, but one in particular was closely tied to the revolution that was to come. A handbill in 1769 urged "the Betrayed Inhabitants of New York" to fight a recent legislative agreement to supply the king's troops—declaring it an affront to American liberty. The legislature branded the handbill a seditious libel and offered a reward for information concerning the identity of its author, signed "Son of Liberty."

The handbill was traced to the print shop of James Parker, who was called before the governor and council, together with his employees. Parker refused to answer any questions be-

Alexander McDougall by Max Rosenthal. The New York Public Library, Astor, Lenox and Tilden Foundations, Emmet Collection

cause he feared he would incriminate himself. Parker's employees, promised immunity if they cooperated, imprisonment if they did not, broke down and identified Captain Alexander McDougall as the author. Parker then admitted his role as printer and McDougall's as author, in return for a pardon.

McDougall was arrested, and his plight quickly became a cause célèbre. The Sons of Liberty orchestrated an extensive campaign on McDougall's behalf that was designed to inflame passions against British oppression. They recognized the opportunity the case presented for gaining public sympathy and support. In the meantime, Parker, the prosecution's key witness, died before the trial could begin. Fearing that the case had fallen apart entirely, the legislature called McDougall before the bar to answer for his crime, but he refused to admit authorship on the basis of his right against self-incrimination. He was returned to jail for contempt of the legislature, since the libel charge could not be made to stick without a confession, or the testimony of a witness. McDougall later went on to serve in the Continental Congress and as a major-general in the Revolutionary War.

Benjamin Franklin by Charles Willson Peale. Franklin chaired the 1776 Pennsylvania Constitutional Convention and was the oldest delegate at the 1787 Federal Convention. The Pennsylvania Academy of The Fine Arts, Philadelphia, Joseph and Sara Harrison Collection

In 1776, many states wrote constitutions, and numbered among their articles a right against self-incrimination—states including Virginia, Pennsylvania, Delaware, Maryland, North Carolina, Vermont, Massachusetts, and New Hampshire. New York and New Jersey merely adopted English common law, which arguably meant that the right was constitutionally recognized in these states as well. It is within these early constitutions that we find language strikingly similar to the provisions covering criminal procedures in the United States Constitution. The 1776 Pennsylvania constitution, written at a convention presided over by Benjamin Franklin, declared:

> IX. That in all prosecutions for criminal offences, a man hath a right to be heard by himself and his council, to demand the cause and nature of his accusation, to be confronted with the witnesses, to call for evidence in his favour, and a speedy public trial, by an impartial jury of the country, without the unanimous consent of which jury he cannot be found guilty; nor can he be compelled to give evidence against himself; nor can any man be justly deprived of his liberty except by the laws of the land, or the judgment of his peers.

The next article in this constitution recited the right against unreasonable search and seizure.

When James Madison introduced the various amendments that were to become the federal Bill of Rights, he included a provision that no one "shall be compelled to be a witness against himself." It was not debated in Congress, although the committee that reported it out added a phrase confining the right to criminal cases.

Confessions resulting from torture are unthinkable in civilized countries today. The Massachusetts charter of 1641, however, did not mark the end of torture as a police procedure, even if it attempted to curtail its use. In the 1930s, a substantial number of cases came up through the courts as a result of lynchings. In *Brown* v. *Mississippi* (1936), the Supreme Court was confronted with a case in which several black defendants had been convicted of murder on the basis of their confessions, and subsequently sentenced to death. The defendants, who were permanently scarred by mistreatment during questioning, claimed the confessions were false and obtained only by the use of torture. One defendant was reportedly hung by a rope from a tree for several brief periods, then tied to the tree and whipped. Afterward, he was released, only to be recaptured a few days later and whipped again until he confessed. The other defendants were stripped, and their "backs were cut to pieces with a leather strap with buckles on it." All the defendants confessed to every detail of the offense as it was put to them. As the whippings continued, they changed their stories as they were asked to do, even in contradictory and equally damaging ways.

Chief Justice Charles Evans Hughes delivered the Supreme Court's opinion in the case of *Brown* v. *Mississippi* (1936), declaring that: "The rack and torture chamber may not be substituted for the witness stand." Collection of the Supreme Court of the United States, Washington, D.C.

Chief Justice Charles Evans Hughes delivered the opinion of the Supreme Court: "The rack and torture chamber may not be substituted for the witness stand." The Court found that torture was prohibited by the Fourteenth Amendment's due process clause.

Self-incrimination was also the issue before the Supreme Court in *Miranda* v. *Arizona* (1966), where Chief Justice Earl Warren wrote the majority opinion:

> The prosecution may not use statements, whether exculpatory or inculpatory, stemming from custodial interrogation of the defendant unless it demonstrates the use of procedural safeguards effective to secure the privilege against self-incrimination. . . . Prior to any questioning, the person must be warned that he has a right to remain silent, that any statement he does make may be used as evidence against him, and that he has a right to the presence of an attorney, either retained or appointed. . . .

Chief Justice Earl Warren. Collection of the Supreme Court of the United States, Washington, D.C.

Chief Justice Warren's opinion is the source of the warnings given a criminal suspect taken into custody today, as well as a standard feature in the scripts of police television dramas.

This benchmark case began when Ernesto Miranda, a seriously disturbed Mexican with pronounced sexual fantasies, was charged with kidnapping and rape. He was interrogated incommunicado for two hours "in a police-dominated atmo-

In 1966, the Supreme Court overturned the conviction of Ernesto A. Miranda (right), for rape and kidnapping on the ground that the police had taken Miranda into custody without advising him of his right to remain silent and consult an attorney. John J. Flynn (left), his attorney, accompanies him in this picture. (Ironically, when Miranda was later killed in a barroom fight, his assailant, Fernando Rodriguez, was read his "Miranda" warnings—in English and Spanish.) Reuters/ Bettmann Newsphotos

Justice George Sutherland wrote the Supreme Court's opinion in *Powell* v. *Alabama* (1932), the "Scottsboro" case, which established the right to have counsel appointed in capital cases. Collection of the Supreme Court of the United States, Washington, D.C.

sphere, resulting in self-incriminating statements without full warnings of his constitutional rights."

Recognizing that psychological ploys rather than physical ones were used to coerce a confession from Miranda, the Court found that the police had deprived the suspect of outside support by interrogating him in private. The "aura of confidence in his guilt undermines his will to resist. He merely confirms the preconceived story the police seek to have him describe. Patience and persistence, at times relentless questioning, are employed." Other strategies, such as false legal advice and "tricks" were standard features in interrogation manuals until this decision.

The *Miranda* requirements do not appear to have lessened the number of confessions police secure through questioning. Some law enforcement officials credit the decision with bringing greater professionalism to police forces, although others resent the emphasis it gives to a suspect's rights.

One part of the *Miranda* warnings covers the right to counsel found in the Sixth Amendment. The "Scottsboro" case, *Powell* v. *Alabama* (1932), which became famous because of the injustices visited upon the defendants, established the right to have counsel appointed in capital cases. The "Scottsboro Boys" (as they were called), nine illiterate young black men, had been convicted of raping "two white girls" on a train. At their arraignment, the trial judge had appointed the whole bar to represent the accused. No one actually stepped in to defend them. As the trial began, a lawyer was appointed without any time to prepare the case. The Supreme Court found that the appointment of an attorney was essential to a fair trial and required under the due process clause of the Fourteenth Amendment. The appointment made in the "Scottsboro" case was inadequate. Justice George Sutherland wrote that the defendants were "young, ignorant, illiterate, surrounded by hostile sentiment, haled back and forth under guard of soldiers, charged with an atrocious crime regarded with especial horror in the community where they were to be tried, and were thus put in peril of their lives within a few moments after counsel . . . began to represent them."

Perhaps the most notable "right-to-counsel" case decided by the Supreme Court is *Gideon* v. *Wainwright* (1963), which inspired a popular book by Anthony Lewis and a television movie starring Henry Fonda. Robert F. Kennedy wrote of the case: "If an obscure Florida convict named Clarence Earl Gideon had not sat down in his prison cell . . . to write a letter to the Supreme Court . . . the vast machinery of American law would have gone on functioning undisturbed. But Gideon did write that letter, the Court did look into his case . . . and the

The Supreme Court found that the "Scottsboro" nine, who were accused of raping two white women, had not been given "due process of law" because their counsel did not have adequate time to prepare a defense. The Court ordered the case to be retried. Here, prior to the retrial, defense lawyer Samuel Leibowitz meets with his clients, Olen Montgomery, Clarence Norris, Willie Roberson, Andrew Wright, Ozie Powell, Eugene Williams, Charley Weems, Roy Wright, and Haywood Patterson. Courtesy Brown Brothers, Sterling, Pennsylvania whole course of American legal history has been changed."

Gideon had been accused of breaking and entering a poolroom with intent to commit a misdemeanor. The crime was a felony. At trial, he asked that an attorney be appointed for him, but his request was denied by the court. He was found guilty and sentenced to five years in jail. Gideon's petition to the Supreme Court asking that his case be reviewed was handwritten in pencil on lined paper. Abe Fortas (later to become a Supreme Court Justice) was appointed to represent Gideon. After the arguments had been heard, the Supreme Court's opinion was delivered by Justice Hugo L. Black who wrote that "reason and reflection require us to recognize that in our adversary system of criminal justice, any person haled into court, who is too poor to hire a lawyer, cannot be assured a fair trial unless counsel is provided for him." The Court thus overturned a 1942 decision and commanded that counsel be provided in all felony cases. In 1972, the right to counsel was expanded to include all criminal cases in which the defendant might be jailed, because a shorter prison sentence for a misdemeanor does not mean the legal case is any less complex. The right to counsel has also been interpreted to require "reasonably competent advice," "effective" assistance of counsel, and representation in the first appeal.

Gideon benefited from the appointment of counsel. After the Supreme Court decision he was retried on the original charges—but this time with representation. His attorney, Fred Turner (now a state judge), built a powerful case against Gideon's principal accuser by skillful cross-examination of the prosecution's witnesses, and unearthing a new witness favorable to his client. The jury found Gideon not guilty.

Once convicted, a defendant still has rights. One of the most important of these rights is the Eighth Amendment's prohibition against "cruel and unusual punishments." The same prohibition appeared in the English Bill of Rights in 1689. Whether a punishment is cruel and unusual is evaluated "from the evolving standards of decency that mark the progress of a maturing society." One of the first cases decided by the Supreme Court in this area, *Weems* v. *United States* (1910), found that punishments grossly excessive in relation to the crime committed, violate the Eighth Amendment.

Paul Weems, a United States government official in the Philippines, was convicted of falsifying pay records and sentenced, under a remnant of Spanish penal law, to fifteen years of hard labor in chains, the permanent loss of political rights, and surveillance by authorities for life. The Supreme Court found the punishment disproportionate to the offense, and therefore unconstitutional.

No. 890 Misc.

DIVISION OF CORRECTIONS

CORRESPONDENCE REGULATIONS

OCT. TERM 1961

U. S. Supreme Court

MAIL WILL NOT BE DELIVERED WHICH DOES NOT CONFORM WITH THESE RULES

No. 1 -- Only 2 letters each week, not to exceed 2 sheets letter-size 8 1/2 x 11" and written *on one side only*, and if ruled paper, do not write between lines. *Your complete name* must be signed at the close of your letter. *Clippings, stamps, letters* from other people, *stationery* or *cash must not be enclosed* in your letters.

No. 2 -- All *letters* must be addressed in the *complete prison name* of the inmate. *Cell number*, where applicable, and *prison number* must be placed in lower left corner of envelope, with your complete name and address in the upper left corner.

No. 3 -- *Do not send any packages without a Package Permit.* Unauthorized *packages* will be destroyed.

No. 4 -- *Letters* must be written in English only.

No. 5 -- *Books, magazines, pamphlets,* and *newspapers* of reputable character will be delivered *only if* mailed direct from the publisher.

No. 6 -- *Money* must be sent in the form of *Postal Money Orders* only, in the inmate's complete prison name and prison number.

RECEIVED
JAN 8 1962
OFFICE OF THE CLERK
SUPREME COURT, U.S.

INSTITUTION ______ CELL NUMBER ______

NAME ______ NUMBER ______

In the Supreme Court of the United States
Washington D.C.
Motion for leave to proceed in Forma Pauperis
Clarence Earl Gideon, Petitioner
VS.
H. G. Cochran Jr, Director, Divisions of corrections State of Florida Respondent

Petitioner Clarence Earl Gideon, who is now held in the Florida state penitentiary, asks leave to file the attached petition for a Writ of Certiorari to the United States Supreme Court, directed to the Supreme Court of The State of Florida, without prepayment of costs and to proceed in Forma Pauperis. The petitioner's affidavit in support is attached hereto.

Clarence Earl Gideon
counsel for Petitioner

Affidavit in support of petition for leave to proceed in Forma Pauperis
Clarence Earl Gideon, petitioner
VS.
H. G. Cochran Jr, Director, Divisions of corrections State of Florida, Respondent.

I, Clarence Earl Gideon, being duly sworn according to law, depose and say that I am

Clarence Earl Gideon's Petition to the Supreme Court of the United States. 1962. National Archives, Washington, D.C.

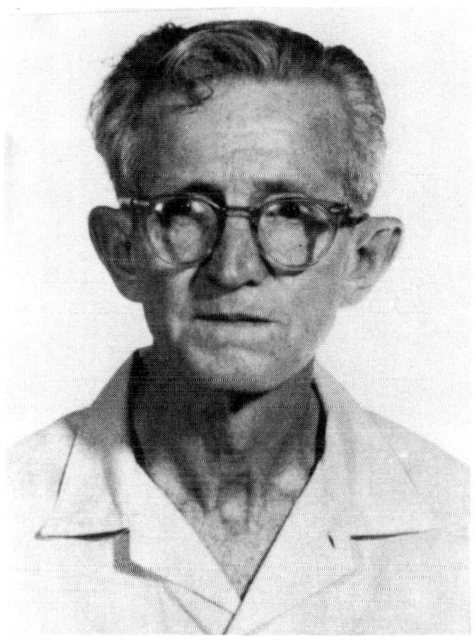

Clarence Earl Gideon. 1963. UPI/Bettmann Newsphotos

Justice Hugo Black, who wrote the Supreme Court's opinion in the case of *Gideon* v. *Wainwright* (1963), noted: ". . . reason and reflection require us to recognize that in our adversary system of criminal justice, any person haled into court, who is too poor to hire a lawyer, cannot be assured a fair trial unless counsel is provided for him." Collection of the Supreme Court of the United States, Washington, D.C.

In *Robinson* v. *California* (1962), the issue was a charge arising under a state law that had made it a crime for a person to be a drug addict, authorizing prosecution "at any time before he reforms." It didn't matter that the suspect had never used or possessed drugs in California—being an addict was enough. The Supreme Court determined that drug addiction—like mental illness, leprosy, or venereal disease—was an illness that "may be contracted innocently or involuntarily. To treat it as a crime constituted cruel and unusual punishment."

Much of the attention paid to the Eighth Amendment in recent years has focused on the death penalty. Justice Potter Stewart explained the Supreme Court's concern here: "The penalty of death differs from all other forms of criminal punishment, not in degree but in kind. It is unique in its total irrevocability. It is unique in its rejection of rehabilitation of the convict as a basic purpose of criminal justice. And it is unique, finally, in its absolute renunciation of all that is embodied in our concept of humanity."

In 1972, the Supreme Court invalidated death penalty statutes that failed to provide sufficient guidance to judges and juries, leaving them unbridled discretion to impose or withhold a penalty of death. Such discretion, the Court said, could lead to death being "so wantonly and so freakishly imposed" as to constitute cruel and unusual punishment. Statutes that specify the aggravating factors upon which a judge or jury could rely in reaching a death penalty decision have been upheld, because only a minority of the Justices believe capital punishment, in and of itself, to be cruel and unusual.

The "cruel and unusual" prohibition has also been applied to prisons, when there has been a denial of adequate medical care, or overcrowded and squalid conditions.

The Constitution, of course, deals with a number of other rights associated with the accused: the prohibition against excessive bail, the protection against double jeopardy, the right to a public trial by an impartial jury, the right of habeas corpus, to name a few. Taken together, they protect the objective of our justice system: fairness. We are all subject to the force of personal prejudices. When someone appears before us dressed too shabbily or too well, is obviously poor or obviously wealthy, is illiterate or well-educated, is an ex-convict or a former hero, the tendency is to prejudge them. This is an aspect of human nature that must be understood by us as it was by the Framers of the Constitution, and applies equally to those individuals who administer the criminal justice system. The Constitution stands as a bulwark that inhibits these prejudices by investing everyone—whatever his or her circumstances—with the rights that a recognition of human dignity requires.

Prisoners on Death Row play a game of chess in a state penitentiary. In 1976, the Supreme Court determined that the death penalty does not always constitute "cruel and unusual punishment." But before imposing it, the sentencing judge or jury must carefully consider the nature of the crime, the character of the offender, and any mitigating circumstances. Photo © Curt Gunther, Camera 5

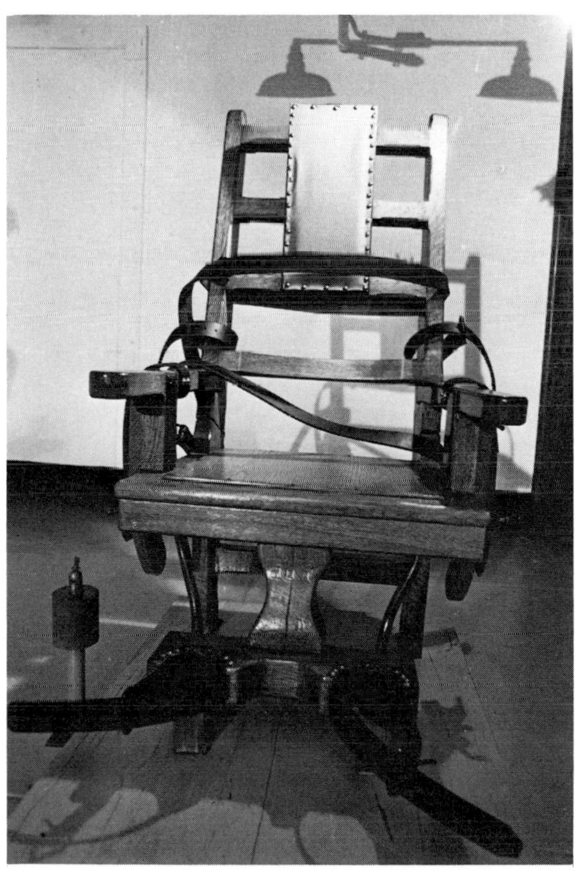

The Electric Chair. Richmond, Virginia. 1982. Understandably, the death penalty remains a highly emotional issue. UPI/Bettmann Newsphotos

We the People of the United States, in Order to form a more perfect Union, establish Justice, insure domestic Tranquility, provide for the common defence, promote the general Welfare, and secure the Blessings of Liberty to ourselves and our Posterity, do ordain and establish this Constitution for the United States of America.

Article. I.

Section. 1. All legislative Powers herein granted shall be vested in a Congress of the United States, which shall consist of a Senate and House of Representatives.

Section. 2. The House of Representatives shall be composed of Members chosen every second Year by the People of the several States, and the Electors in each State shall have the Qualifications requisite for Electors of the most numerous Branch of the State Legislature.

No Person shall be a Representative who shall not have attained to the Age of twenty five Years, and been seven Years a Citizen of the United States, and who shall not, when elected, be an Inhabitant of that State in which he shall be chosen.

Representatives and direct Taxes shall be apportioned among the several States which may be included within this Union, according to their respective Numbers, which shall be determined by adding to the whole Number of free Persons, including those bound to Service for a Term of Years, and excluding Indians not taxed, three fifths of all other Persons. The actual Enumeration shall be made within three Years after the first Meeting of the Congress of the United States, and within every subsequent Term of ten Years, in such Manner as they shall by Law direct. The Number of Representatives shall not exceed one for every thirty Thousand, but each State shall have at Least one Representative; and until such enumeration shall be made, the State of New Hampshire shall be entitled to chuse three, Massachusetts eight, Rhode-Island and Providence Plantations one, Connecticut five, New-York six, New Jersey four, Pennsylvania eight, Delaware one, Maryland six, Virginia ten, North Carolina five, South Carolina five, and Georgia three.

When vacancies happen in the Representation from any State, the Executive Authority thereof shall issue Writs of Election to fill such Vacancies.

The House of Representatives shall chuse their Speaker and other Officers; and shall have the sole Power of Impeachment.

Section. 3. The Senate of the United States shall be composed of two Senators from each State, chosen by the Legislature thereof for six Years; and each Senator shall have one Vote.

Immediately after they shall be assembled in Consequence of the first Election, they shall be divided as equally as may be into three Classes. The Seats of the Senators of the first Class shall be vacated at the Expiration of the second Year, of the second Class at the Expiration of the fourth Year, and of the third Class at the Expiration of the sixth Year, so that one third may be chosen every second Year; and if Vacancies happen by Resignation, or otherwise, during the Recess of the Legislature of any State, the Executive thereof may make temporary Appointments until the next Meeting of the Legislature, which shall then fill

PART IV

Governing A Nation

The Constitution of the United States was signed in Philadelphia on September 17, 1787, and ratified in 1788. Shown here are the Preamble to the Constitution and the beginning of Article I. Library of Congress, Washington, D.C.

The Constitution of the United States of America is an experiment in self-government that assumes citizens will be knowledgeable about public affairs and take responsibility for helping to shape policy. Too often, however, we pay little heed to public policy issues until they suddenly rear up in our own backyard. That is what happened to the people in a small cluster of communities in central New Hampshire when they learned the Energy Department had proposed the establishment of a nuclear waste dump site in the midst of their farmland. To the inhabitants of Hillsborough, it seemed as though a remote authority was planning to seize their land and change their lives, apparently without any concern for their wishes in the matter.

Naturally, the townspeople gathered to discuss the problem. More than one thousand residents met in a high school gymnasium to explore ways to fight the dump. In doing so, they were participating in a tradition dating back to March 14, 1743, when the first town meeting in America was held at Boston's Faneuil Hall. Since then, the American passion for discussion of public issues has never waned. By many, it is even considered a civic responsibility. As Justice Louis D. Brandeis wrote in 1927: "Those who won our independence believed

. . . that public discussion is a political duty; and that this should be a fundamental principle of the American government."

Discussion, however, is only the first step in the process—a prelude to some form of concerted action. Led by a former teamster organizer, Gerry Dubrino, the people of Hillsborough organized a convoy of 318 huge tractor-trailers that converged on Concord, the state capital, in the driving rain. Although the Hillsborough communities succeeded in winning support from the state for their position, the decision rests in the hands of the federal government—no matter how much the state may protest. The Supreme Court has recognized that the federal government has preeminent authority over health and safety issues where nuclear energy is concerned (although state regulation of related economic activities is permitted). Thus, the Court has affirmed its finding that the Supremacy Clause makes the Constitution, and all laws passed pursuant to it, the "supreme law of the land." The people of Hillsborough must try to work for a political, rather than a legal, solution to their problem. If they can generate sufficient protest against the dump site and sufficient sympathy for their cause, the political price of the dump may be too high for the federal government to pay, even if it has the constitutional power to impose its will on New Hampshire.

It was when no political solution seemed to offer the colonials relief from a series of increasingly onerous British edicts that the American Revolution began. Overall, the colonies had prospered under British rule. Although there were trade restrictions, the colonies had generally evaded them without incurring substantial penalties. In the aftermath of the French and Indian War, with their enemies to the north no longer a threat, the colonies had looked forward to an era of renewed prosperity. The British, however, needed revenues to satisfy the debts incurred during that war, as well as to finance their other obligations as a world power. They imposed taxes on the colonies, first in the form of a Sugar Act in 1764—which also cut off the illegal but profitable West Indies trade—followed by a Stamp Act in 1765. Violators of these Acts were tried without a jury, for juries made up of fellow Americans were likely to have been sympathetic to anyone accused of smuggling or evading taxes. Harsher measures followed, challenged by the colonials, who maintained that "taxation without representation is tyranny." Finally, the breach between the British and Americans proved irreparable, and a revolution that would ultimately separate the American colonies from the British empire ensued.

Having won their independence against tremendous odds,

Town Meeting. 1795. New England Town Meetings were direct descendants of the traditions brought by the Pilgrims to the New World—and not always peaceful affairs. The New York Public Library, Astor, Lenox and Tilden Foundations

In response to the Stamp Act, Massachusetts called a meeting in New York of the other colonies "to implore relief." The resolutions of the 1765 Stamp Act Congress were an important early step on the road to independence. The Newberry Library, Chicago

Join, or Die by Benjamin Franklin. 1754. The New York Public Library, Astor, Lenox and Tilden Foundations

the thirteen former colonies recognized that their strength lay in some form of confederation. Still, the young revolutionaries we call our Founding Fathers were Virginians, New Yorkers, and Pennsylvanians first—Americans second. They had just overthrown an oppressive centralized government and were determined to avoid its re-creation.

Although there were some Americans who favored the establishment of a monarchy with George Washington as king, most viewed the Revolution as a complete repudiation of royal authority and a victory for the then-radical ideology of republicanism. A republic is an elected form of representative government dedicated to the welfare of the people, rather than to the personal desires of the rulers. It relies upon what James Madison was to call "the genius of the people" and requires a population educated in the values of individual worth and dignity. To achieve those ideals and create a sense of nationhood, however, was to prove a most difficult task.

The Founders were convinced that a written charter was essential to establish a nation dedicated to the "self-evident" truths that had been the clarion call of the Revolution. But it took four years to achieve the unanimous consent necessary for ratification of their first attempt—the Articles of Confederation. While that agreement was an achievement in itself, the Articles proved unworkable as a formula for governance. Instead, they merely linked the states in a "firm league of friendship" that called upon them to act in concert for "their common defence, the security of their liberties, and their mutual and general welfare."

Under the Confederation, there was no president or unifying leadership. Congress, the embodiment of the national government, was denied the power to tax or to regulate commerce. As a result, insolvency plagued the new nation, and Revolutionary War veterans threatened insurrection over the pensions they had been promised, but were never paid. The Treaty of Paris, which had ended the American Revolution, went unenforced, since Congress was powerless to dislodge British frontier posts from United States soil.

The American nation could not survive under the Articles of Confederation; it provided no effective means of response to a variety of national crises. The brief period of prosperity experienced after independence had been won gave way to a severe depression. Taxes—imposed by the states to pay the war debt—had risen steeply. Farmers in western Massachusetts, who had served as soldiers, saw their cattle, their plows, and even their farms confiscated to satisfy unpaid debts. Calling themselves "Regulators," these ex-soldiers—often dressed in their old Revolutionary War uniforms—crowded into court-

John Dickinson chaired a committee that drafted Articles of Confederation shortly after Independence was declared on July 4, 1776. For over a year, the draft lay dormant except for occasional debate. A substantially revised document, with considerably less power vested in the governing Congress, was approved on November 15, 1777. Virginia and New York (destined to become two of the last ratifiers of the Constitution) were the first to ratify the Articles of Confederation, but unanimous ratification of the Articles was not achieved until March 1, 1781. Photograph by Jonathan Wallen. National Archives, Washington, D.C.

A broadside, apparently issued during Daniel Shays's march on Springfield, Massachusetts, in 1787, depicts Shays and Job Shattuck, another leader of Shays's Rebellion. The accompanying verse expresses the hope that Shays will be successful in preventing a court from sitting at Springfield to indict the rebels, and that Shattuck will soon be released from prison. National Portrait Gallery, Smithsonian Institution

George Washington's home at Mount Vernon was the site of an early interstate meeting to resolve the crisis in commerce that eventually led to the Constitutional Convention. Some states, James Madison wrote, "having no convenient ports for foreign commerce, were subject to be taxed by their neighbors. . . . New Jersey, placed between Philadelphia and New York, was likened to a cask tapped at both ends; and North Carolina, between Virginia and South Carolina, to a patient bleeding at both arms." The Mount Vernon Ladies' Association, Mount Vernon, Virginia

The Convention at Philadelphia in 1787 met behind closed doors, and the delegates were pledged to secrecy. After they completed their task in September, a citizen asked Benjamin Franklin what kind of government the delegates had devised. "A republic," he replied, "if you can keep it." Library of Congress, Washington, D.C.

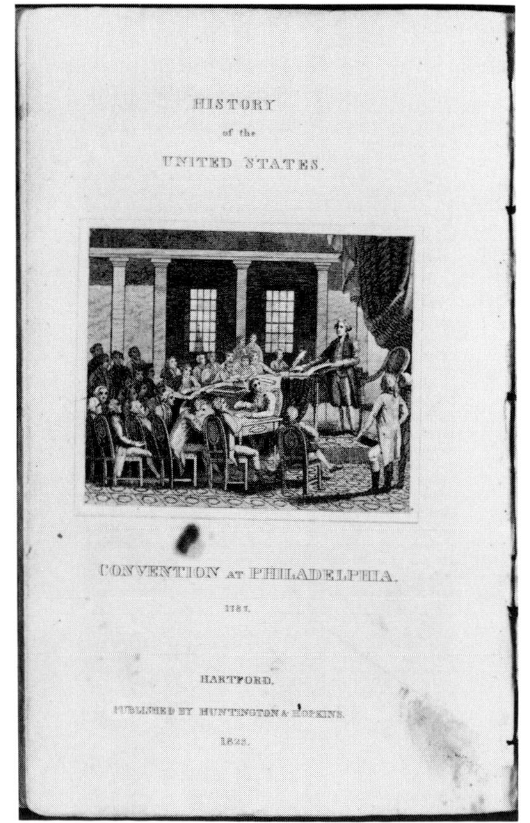

HISTORY
of the
UNITED STATES.

CONVENTION AT PHILADELPHIA.
1787.

HARTFORD.
PUBLISHED BY HUNTINGTON & HOPKINS.
1823.

houses hundreds at a time, interrupting legal proceedings against debtors in a way that judges and sheriffs were powerless to halt. Rumors of insurrection in Massachusetts were commonplace. In January 1787, Daniel Shays actually led more than one thousand men in an unsuccessful assault on an arsenal in that state.

Shays's Rebellion was an expression of extreme frustration with the unfulfilled promises of independence. The Massachusetts farmers, faced with the specter of deepening poverty, felt that the oppression of the king had merely been replaced with a tyranny of laws manipulated by rich Bostonians. States, too, experienced frustration in trying to deal with one another. Virginia and Maryland called a meeting in March 1785 to confront some of their problems. With George Washington presiding, the Mount Vernon Commercial Conference settled some nettlesome disputes between those states over navigational rights on the Potomac. Its success led Virginia to call a second meeting on issues of commerce and trade, to which all thirteen states were invited. The Annapolis Convention of 1786, however, was not similarly successful. Although nine states appointed delegates (the host state, Maryland, did not), only twelve men representing five states actually attended. Still, the Annapolis delegates issued a call for a convention to be held in the city of Philadelphia in May of 1787 "to render the constitution of the Federal Government adequate to the exigencies of the union."

While Shays and his followers prepared another assault upon the arsenal, a concerned Continental Congress, on February 21, 1787, authorized a Philadelphia convention "for the sole and express purpose of revising the Articles of Confederation." Seventy-four delegates were named to the Convention, although only fifty-five would ultimately attend. Several prominent Americans refused to serve as delegates. Patrick Henry, for example, refused the honor because he "smelt a rat." Rhode Island declined to participate altogether and sent no delegates. An eager James Madison was the first to arrive, some ten days before the next delegate. The Convention, called for May 14, did not begin until May 25 when a quorum was finally present in the Pennsylvania State House, now known as Independence Hall.

As the first order of business, George Washington was unanimously elected presiding officer. William Jackson, who was not a delegate, was elected to serve as secretary. The assembled delegates struggled to reconcile tremendously antithetical concerns: the fear that a centralized government would naturally lead to oppression, balanced against the desperate need for a strong national government; the fulfillment

Edmund Randolph. Virginia State Library, Richmond

of democratic ideals, against an apprehension that a popular majority could sweep away the rights of a powerless minority; principles of equality in political representation, against the protection of smaller states from domination by the larger ones; and the goal of universal freedom, against the southern states' commitment to the institution of slavery.

It didn't take long for the delegates to outdistance their mandate from Congress and reject the Articles of Confederation entirely in favor of a wholly new constitution. Just four days after they had assembled, Virginia Governor Edmund Randolph proposed a plan, written primarily by James Madison, to establish an "energetic" national government consisting of a bicameral legislature, an executive branch, and a system of federal courts. Under this proposal, one house of the legislature was to be elected by the people, with representation distributed among the states in relation to population, while the second house was to be elected by the first. The legislature was also to have the power to invalidate state laws.

The Virginia Plan caused widespread turmoil throughout the Convention. Many delegates thought the power to negate state laws was the equivalent of abolishing the states. On June 15, however, William Paterson of New Jersey offered an alternative to the Virginia Plan—one featuring a single-house Congress in which all states would be equally represented. While the debate over congressional representation was so vociferous that it brought threats of walkouts and even disunion, the New Jersey Plan accepted the principal tenet of Madison's original blueprint: a stronger national government capable of enacting and enforcing laws that would be binding upon all the states, and having a direct relationship to the people, not just the states. Despite this broad area of agreement, the Convention appeared deadlocked and, as Gouverneur Morris of Pennsylvania later remarked, "the fate of America was suspended by a hair." A compromise proposal generally credited to the Connecticut delegation established an upper chamber with equal representation for all the states, and a lower chamber with proportional representation. The upper chamber was to consist of senators selected by state legislatures to ensure the preservation of state prerogatives. (This selection process was replaced by direct election of senators when the Seventeenth Amendment was adopted in 1913.) With the question of representation settled, it was easier to reach agreement on other issues.

Nevertheless, there was no lack of strong opinions on almost every issue. How would the president be elected? What powers would the states accept in a national congress? The wording of every phrase of the final document began to assume heightened importance. Even the Constitution's Preamble,

1. Resolved, that the articles of the Confed.ⁿ ought to be so corrected and enlarged, as to accomplish the objects proposed by their institution, namely, "common defence, security of liberty, and general welfare."

2. Resolved therefore, that the rights of suffrage in the national legislature ought to be proportioned to the quotas of contribution, or to the number of free inhabitants, as the one or the other may seem best, in different cases. [Postponed.]

3. Resolved, that the national legislature ought to consist of two branches.

4. Resolved, that the members of the first branch of the national leg.ᵉ ought to be elected by the people of the several States every ____ for the term of ____ to be of the age of ____ years at least. to receive liberal stipends, by which they may be compensated for the devotion of their time to public service. to be ineligible to any office established by a particular State, or under the authority of the U. S. (except those peculiarly belonging to the functions of the first branch) during the term of service and for the space of ____ after its expiration; to be incapable of re-election for the space of ____ after the expiration of their term of service, and to be subjected to recal. [Postponed.]

5. Resolved, that the members of the second branch of the national leg. ought to be elected by those of the first, out of a proper number of persons nominated by the individual legislatures; to be of the age of ____ years at least; to hold their offices for a term sufficient to ensure their independency; to receive liberal stipends by which they may be compensated for the devotion of their time to the public service; and to be ineligible to any office established by a particular [Not passed.]

Excerpt from a working copy of the Virginia Plan. May 29, 1787. Library of Congress, Washington, D.C.

Gouverneur Morris and Robert Morris by Charles Willson Peale. 1783. Robert Morris (right) had helped to finance the American Revolution, but would die penniless. Gouverneur Morris (left) was largely responsible for the final language used in the Constitution. Pennsylvania Academy of the Fine Arts, Philadelphia

which is regarded as having no legal effect, was the subject of revision, because of the initial impression it would convey. Originally, it was proposed that it should begin, "We the People of and the States of New Hampshire, Massachusetts, Rhode Island . . . " But there were those who thought that this gave undue importance to the people over the states. A revised version emerged as, "We the People of the States of . . . " Only because no one could confidently predict which states would finally subscribe to the Constitution did Gouverneur Morris's simple phrase prevail: "We the People of the United States . . . "

The spirit of compromise that prevailed on the issue of representation continued throughout the Convention. Some of these compromises—most notably the one concerning slavery—were to come undone in the future. However, the art of compromise practiced at the Convention was to become one of the great hallmarks of the American political system and one of the reasons for its continued survival.

As the Framers negotiated to craft a Constitution acceptable to the various states, they relied upon not only the wisdom of elder statesmen such as Benjamin Franklin, but also upon the power of ideas expostulated by a long line of political theorists. In fact, the Constitution has sometimes been characterized as the climax of the Enlightenment—the eighteenth-century attempt to apply the results of Western scientific discoveries and learning to human affairs. Its theoretical strands stretched from John Locke, David Hume, and Baron de Montesquieu back to classical antiquity. The Founding Fathers thus combined an inspiration based upon lofty intellectual philosophies and theories with a pragmatism honed during colonial settlement and revolutionary battles. The first colonists came to the New World relying on charters that also provided them with their initial laws. Upon winning their independence, each of the states had endeavored to write a constitution, many of which shared principles concerning the dispersal of power and the preservation of liberty—although often in strikingly dissimilar ways. Still, the state constitutional experiences were invaluable to the Framers, and assisted them in completing their task of writing a federal constitution over a short four-month period.

During the Convention, James Madison was most vehement in stating his belief that the final form of government should be republican in nature. He collected nearly two hundred histories of prior confederations as "beacons, which give warning of the course to be shunned, without pointing out that which ought to be pursued." It was in defense of republicanism that Madison rose to his greatest literary and oratorical

Monday Sepr. 17. 1787. In Convention

The engrossed Constitution being read,

Docr. Franklin rose with a ~~written~~ speech in his hand, which he had reduced to writing for his own conveniency, and which Mr. Wilson read in the words following.

Mr. President

I confess that there are several parts of this constitution which I do not at present approve, but I am not sure I shall never approve them: For having lived long, I have experienced many instances of being obliged by better information or fuller consideration, to change opinions even on important subjects, which I once thought right, but found to be otherwise. It is therefore that the older I grow, the more apt I am to doubt my own judgement, and to pay more respect to the judgement of others. Most men indeed as well as most sects in Religion, think themselves in possession of all truth, and that wherever others differ from them it is so far error. Steele a Protestant in a Dedication tells the Pope, that the only difference between our Churches in their opinions of the certainty of their doctrines is, the Church of Rome is infallible and the Church of England is never in the wrong. But though many private persons think almost as highly of their own infallibility as of that of their sect, few express it so naturally as a certain french lady, who in a dispute with her sister, said "I don't know how it happens, Sister but I meet with no body but myself, that's always in the right — Il n'y a que moi qui a toujours raison."

In these sentiments, Sir, I agree to this Constitution with all its faults, if they are such; because I think a general Government necessary for us, and there is no form of Government but what may be a blessing to the people if well administered, and believe farther that this is likely to be well administered for a course of years, and can only end in Despotism, as other forms have done before it, when the people shall become so corrupted as to need despotic Government, being incapable of any other. I doubt too whether any other Conven-tion

James Madison was perhaps one of those most responsible for the success of the Constitutional Convention. He came prepared with the proposals known as the Virginia Plan, and he rose to speak 161 times. His notes on each day's proceedings provide the best record of what transpired behind the Convention's closed doors. Library of Congress, Washington, D.C.

Howard Chandler Christy's rendition of the signing of the Constitution of the United States, is a mural in the United States Capitol. Architect of the Capitol, Washington, D.C.

heights. A republic, he asserted, allowed the public views to be refined and enlarged "by passing them through the medium of a chosen body of citizens, whose wisdom may best discern the true interest of their country, and whose patriotism and love of justice, will be least likely to sacrifice it to temporary or partial considerations." He saw the incipient American republic as the model for the rest of mankind.

On September 17, 1787, an engrossed copy of the Constitution was placed before the delegates. With only Edmund Randolph, George Mason, and Elbridge Gerry declining, the remaining thirty-nine delegates, one by one, came forward to sign the document. As the last delegates signed, Benjamin Franklin observed that he had often wondered during the sessions whether the half-sun painted on the President's chair occupied by George Washington was rising or setting. "But now at length," he said, "I have the happiness to know that it is a rising and not a setting Sun."

The 1787 Constitution, even with all the compromises it contained to satisfy the assembled delegates, did not command immediate acceptance outside the Convention. The Antifederalists opposed the charter for granting too much power to the central government and thus enfeebling the states. They saw the Constitution as a potential instrument of tyranny. Virginian Richard Henry Lee asserted that the government as formulated would transfer power "from the many to

Rising Sun Chair occupied by George Washington during the Constitutional Convention. Courtesy of the Independence National Historical Park Collection, Philadelphia

Detail of the Rising Sun Chair

Richard Henry Lee of Virginia. Courtesy of the Independence National Historical Park Collection, Philadelphia

Alexander Hamilton. Courtesy Art Commission of the City of New York

the few." Among the Antifederalists were men who had earned substantial followings during the fight for independence, men such as Virginians Patrick Henry and George Mason. They charged that no federal republic could govern a territory so vast, and that the omission of a bill of rights was evidence of intent on the part of some to reverse the outcome of the Revolution. The Antifederalists may have lost their battle against the Constitution when they decided to fight its ratification, rather than contest its underlying legality. After all, the Convention had been authorized only to propose amendments (which would have required unanimous consent for adoption) to the Articles of Confederation, not to draft an entirely new charter. The Antifederalist cause was further weakened by their failure to propose an alternative to the Constitution.

However, their lasting achievement was to build support for the addition of a bill of rights to the Constitution as originally presented for ratification. Among the concerns of the Antifederalists were the common law protections of the right to a jury trial, freedom from unreasonable searches and seizures, and the unlawfulness of cruel and unusual punishment. In addition, they spoke out eloquently on behalf of freedom of the press and freedom of conscience.

While Delaware acted almost immediately to ratify the Constitution, many state legislatures debated the issue long and heatedly, eventually ratifying the new charter by a close margin. To support the cause of ratification in New York, many newspapers there published a series of letters written under the pseudonym "Publius" during the period from October 27, 1787 to May 28, 1788. Issued in book form a year later, *The Federalist*, written by Alexander Hamilton, James Madison, and John Jay, was a brilliant exposition of political theory, arguing that the failure of the Articles of Confederation had created a power vacuum that could only be filled by an energetic government deriving its power from the consent of the people and dedicated to the cause of individual liberty. Although *The Federalist* was a compelling form of political rhetoric, it also remains an important source used by the courts to interpret the Constitution's meaning.

On June 21, 1788, New Hampshire became the ninth state to ratify the Constitution, thus providing the necessary approval of three-quarters of the states. However, two of the largest states, Virginia and New York, had not yet ratified the governing charter. Without the approval of these two key states, both populous and pivotal in terms of commerce, the nation might not have survived. In Virginia, James Madison outdebated Patrick Henry and George Mason—approval there was won by a vote of eighty-nine to seventy-nine. Alexander

New-York, *Nov.* 22.

The Monument erected in this city, to the memory of that patriotic warrior, the late General MONTGOMERY, has received the following elegant ornamental additions, designed by Major L'Enfant, the gentleman to whom we are indebted for superintending its original erection:—"Hymen, extinguishing his torch, mourns over the tomb. From behind the pyramid rises a Sun with thirteen rays, which enlightens the quarter of a terrestrial globe, emblematical of America. Above the whole is the American Eagle flying from East to West, carrying in his talons a starry curtain, in which the globe appears to have been wrapped." It must give real satisfaction to every patriotic mind, to behold the attention of genius and taste thus generously employed, in celebrating American heroism and departed virtue.

A Liverpool paper of the 24th Sept. says, "It is not improbable, after all the endeavors of the mediating powers, but that the States of Holland, West Frizeland, and Utrecht, will oblige the King of Prussia to proceed to extremities, as he may think proper, in vindication of the Stadtholder's rights, and to restore the ancient Constitution of the Republic, now broken and divided by the many jarring resolves of the above-mentioned States. We confess we have our doubts of the probability of the French assisting the States; and it is even confessed by the political intelligencers on the patriot side, that the system of the Court of France is changed on this head, and that they are to try every method in the way of mediation first, and appease, if possible, instead of irritating the Prussian Monarch.

"It puzzles the brain of the wisest politician to devise what kind of satisfaction France can offer, or Prussia accept, other than that which is impossible, viz. a disavowal of the attempt to seize the Princess of Orange, and the punishment of those who did make that attempt. This the States can never submit to, without violating their faith to their supporters——and violating truth at the same time; for it is well known, and they cannot deny it, that the Princess has long been the object of their aversion. It is more than four years since they openly accused her of intriguing politically against the States; and, when the Prince demanded satisfaction for this insult, they refused to prosecute the Printers of such libels.

"In fact, it may be said of Holland as it was said of America, 'The design to be independent did not, in the latter case, take its rise from the Tea Act. It had before that period risen to a very considerable height. That was the pretence only. And in Holland, for a series of years, jealousies have been encouraged and fomented by the Aristocratic and Democratic parties against the Monarchial or Stadtholderian party. Real injuries never were complained of. But surmises, insinuations, and allegations, were made without number, and an aversion to the Stadtholder's person, family, and Government, is at the bottom of every proceeding since the American war.——At that time the Dutch furnished the Americans with every necessary for carrying on the war against Britain, contrary to the faith of nations. When, in consequence of many fruitless remonstrances, we were impelled to do ourselves justice, the Dutch, from the hesitating and slow form of their Constitution, were unprepared, and throughout the whole war unsuccessful. They accused the Stadtholder as being in secret combination with England; they proved nothing, even after the long enquiry into the affair of the Brest fleet. But although they proved nothing, they have gone on ever since *suspecting*; and we believe that if many, who are now most inveterate against the Stadtholder, were to be asked this plain question, *What has he done*? they would be at a loss to make an answer.—Hence it is, that no nation will adopt the cause of the Dutch, unless from interested views, for to the *pity* of any nation they have no claim. And all that the philosopher and the philanthropist can do is, to brood over the impending calamities of a civil war, and to regret that a country that might be happy and flourishing, is like to be deluged in blood."

On the 24th of August, in lat. 45. 46, N. long. 38. 0, W. Capt. Collinson (of the Backhouse, which arrived at Liverpool on the 23d Sept. from Grenada) being about a mile astern of a French East-Indiaman, which was bound for L'Orient, perceived a man floating on the water towards him; on which he threw an oar and an empty cask overboard, for present assistance, and got his boat out as soon as possible, with which he was fortunate enough to get him on board his vessel. On questioning him, he learned that he was one of three men, who, for some misbehaviour, had been sentenced, in the East-Indies, to be sent to Old France, and there shot to death by way of example; when, seeing the Backhouse so near, and being released from the irons with which he had been for a long time confined, impelled by that natural love of life which is implanted in our nature, he took the resolution of getting out of one of the port-holes, and dropping into the water, chusing to run the risque of drowning, rather than proceed to his native country, where certain death awaited him; and this risque was very great, as he seemed to know little more of swimming, than just to keep himself above water; for tho' the oar, which was thrown overboard, came within five yards, he seemed not to know how to get nearer to it.

In the Liverpool papers, the Eliza, Mercer, and the Betsey and Amey, Watt, are advertised for New-York;

The Hall, Ward, for Philadelphia;

The Irish Volunteer, Cooke, for Baltimore;

The Peace and Plenty, Williams, for Boston;

The Henderson, Steel, and the Abby, Braithwaite, for James River,

The Anne, Tolson; Clio, Dawson; Jane, Watson; and Ardeer, Sutherland; for Charleston.

They were all to sail early in October.

Extracts from English Prints received per the Hector, from Liverpool.

L O N D O N.

Sept. 11. Mr. Grenville is returned to the Continent, with full powers for executing the negociation now on the tapis between his Majesty and the Prince of Orange.

An anonymous correspondent says, he has received a letter from Holland, dated August 28, which states, that by accounts from Rotterdam it appears, that the Prince of Brunswick had received a wound in a skirmish near Utrecht, which the surgeons had declared mortal; and that great alarm was spread in consequence of this affair.

One of the principal articles of the late Convention between France and England is, "That no ships of war, of any description, on either side, shall sail for the East-Indies, without mutual consent." This article will, in all probability, be one of the best preservatives against war, as it has been the policy of France, for near half a century, to strengthen herself, previous to a rupture, in her extra European settlements. She did so in the West-Indies in the war of 1744; in America in the war of 1756; and in the East-Indies in the late war, just before she declared in favor of America.

The following is the 13th article in the Definitive Treaty of Peace, to which the Convention announced in the Gazette alludes: "Art. XIII. If either of the high contracting parties has granted, or shall grant, any bounties for encouraging the [illegible] growth, produce, or manufacture of his dominions, the other party shall be allowed to add, to the duties imposed by virtue of the present treaty, on the said goods and merchandize imported into his dominions, such an import duty as shall be equivalent to said bounty. But this stipulation is not to be extended to cases of restoration of duties and imposts (called draw-backs) which are allowed upon exportation."

The FEDERALIST, No. X.

To the People of the State of New-York.

AMONG the numerous advantages promised by a well constructed Union, none deserves to be more accurately developed than its tendency to break and control the violence of faction. The friend of popular governments, never finds himself so much alarmed for their character and fate, as when he contemplates their propensity to this dangerous vice. He will not fail therefore to set a due value on any plan which, without violating the principles to which he is attached, provides a proper cure for it. The instability, injustice and confusion introduced into the public councils, have in truth been the mortal diseases under which popular governments have every where perished; as they continue to be the favorite and fruitful topics from which the adversaries to liberty derive their most specious declamations. The valuable improvements made by the American Constitutions on the popular models, both ancient and modern, cannot certainly be too much admired; but it would be an unwarrantable partiality, to contend that they have as effectually obviated the danger on this side as was wished and expected. Complaints are every where heard from our most considerate and virtuous citizens, equally the friends of public and private faith, and of public and personal liberty; that our governments are too unstable; that the public good is disregarded in the conflicts of rival parties; and that measures are too often decided, not according to the rules of justice, and the rights of the minor party; but by the superior force of an interested and over-bearing majority. However anxiously we may wish that these complaints had no foundation, the evidence of known facts will not permit us to deny that they are in some degree true. It will be found indeed, on a candid review of our situation, that some of the distresses under which we labor, have been erroneously charged on the operation of our governments; but it will be found, at the same time, that other causes will not alone account for many of our heaviest misfortunes; and particularly, for that prevailing and increasing distrust of public engagements, and alarm for private rights, which are echoed from one end of the continent to the other. These must be chiefly, if not wholly, effects of the unsteadiness and injustice, with which a factious spirit has tainted our public administrations.

By a faction I understand a number of citizens, whether amounting to a majority or minority of the whole, who are united and actuated by some common impulse of passion, or of interest, adverse to the rights of other citizens, or to the permanent and aggregate interests of the community.

There are two methods of curing the mischiefs of faction: the one, by removing its causes; the other, by controling its effects.

There are again two methods of removing the causes of faction: the one by destroying the liberty which is essential to its existence; the other, by giving to every citizen the same opinions, the same passions, and the same interests.

It could never be more truly said than of the first remedy, that it is worse than the disease. Liberty is to faction, what air is to fire, an aliment without which it instantly expires. But it could not be a less folly to abolish liberty, which is essential to political life, because it nourishes faction, than it would be to wish the annihilation of air, which is essential to animal life, because it imparts to fire its destructive agency.

The second expedient is as impracticable, as the first would be unwise. As long as the reason of man continues fallible, and he is at liberty to exercise it, different opinions will be formed. As long as the connection subsists between his reason and his self-love, his opinions and his passions will have a reciprocal influence on each other; and the former will be objects to which the latter will attach themselves. The diversity in the faculties of men from which the rights of property originate, is not less an insuperable obstacle to a uniformity of interests. The protection of these faculties is the first object of Government. From the protection of different and unequal faculties of acquiring property, the possession of different degrees and kinds of property immediately results: and from the influence of these on the sentiments and views of the respective proprietors, ensues a division of the society into different interests and parties.

The latent causes of faction are thus sown in the nature of man; and we see them every where brought into different degrees of activity, according to the different circumstances of civil society. A zeal for different opinions concerning religion, concerning Government and many other points, as well of speculation as of practice; an attachment to different leaders ambitiously contending for pre-eminence and power; or to persons of other descriptions whose fortunes have been interesting to the human passions, have in turn divided mankind into parties, inflamed them with mutual animosity, and rendered them much more disposed to vex and oppress each other, than to co-operate for their common good. So strong is this propensity of mankind to fall into mutual animosities, that where no substantial occasion presents itself, the most frivolous and fanciful distinctions have been sufficient to kindle their unfriendly passions, and excite their most violent conflicts. But the most common and durable source of factions, has been the various and unequal distribution of property. Those who hold, and those who are without property, have ever formed distinct interests in society. Those who are creditors, and those who are debtors, fall under a like discrimination. A landed interest, a manufacturing interest, a mercantile interest, a monied interest, with many lesser interests, grow up of necessity in civilized nations, and divide them into different classes, actuated by different sentiments and views. The regulation of these various and interfering interests forms the principal task of modern Legislation, and involves the spirit of party and faction in the necessary and ordinary operations of Government.

No man is allowed to be a judge in his own cause; because his interest would certainly bias his judgment, and, not improbably, corrupt his integrity. With equal, nay with greater reason, a body of men, are unfit to be both judges and parties, at the same time; yet, what are many of the most important acts of legislation, but so many judicial determinations, not indeed concerning the rights of single persons, but concerning the rights of large bodies of citizens; and what are the different classes of legislators, but advocates and parties to the causes which they determine? Is a law proposed concerning private debts? It is a question to which the creditors are parties on one side, and the debtors on the other. Justice ought to hold the balance between them. Yet the parties are and must be themselves the judges; and the most numerous party, or, in other words, the most powerful faction must be expected to prevail. Shall domestic manufactures be encouraged, and in what degree, by restrictions on foreign manufactures? are questions which would be differently decided by the landed and the manufacturing classes; and probably by neither, with a sole regard to justice and the public good. The apportionment of taxes on the various descriptions of property, is an act which seems to require the most exact impartiality; yet there is perhaps no legislative act in which greater opportunity and temptation are given to a predominant party, to trample on the rules of justice. Every shilling with which they over-burden the inferior number, is a shilling saved to their own pockets.

It is in vain to say, that enlightened statesmen will be able to adjust these clashing interests, and render them all subservient to the public good. Enlightened statesmen will not always be at the helm: Nor, in many cases, can such an adjustment be made at all, without taking into view indirect and remote considerations, which will rarely prevail over the immediate interest which one party may find in disregarding the rights of another, or the good of the whole.

The inference to which we are brought, is, that the *causes* of faction cannot be removed; and that relief is only to be sought in the means of controling its *effects*.

If a faction consists of less than a majority, relief is supplied by the republican principle, which enables the majority to defeat its sinister views by regular vote: It may clog the administration, it may convulse the society; but it will be unable to execute and mask its violence under the forms of the Constitution. When a majority is included in a faction, the form of popular government on the other hand enables it to sacrifice to its ruling passion or interest, both the public good and the rights of other citizens. To secure the public good, and private rights, against the danger of such a faction, and at the same time to preserve the spirit and the form of popular government, is then the great object to which our enquiries are directed: Let me add that it is the great desideratum, by which alone this form of government can be rescued from the opprobrium under which it has so long labored, and be recommended to the esteem and adoption of mankind.

By what means is this object attainable? Evidently by one of two only. Either the existence of the same passion or interest in a majority at the same time, must be prevented; or the majority, having such co-existent passion or interest, must be rendered, by their number and local situation, unable to concert and carry into effect schemes of oppression. If the impulse and the opportunity be suffered to coincide, we well know that neither moral nor religious motives can be relied on as an adequate control. They are not found to be such on the injustice and violence of individuals, and lose their efficacy in proportion to the number combined together; that is, in proportion as their efficacy becomes needful.

From this view of the subject, it may be concluded, that a pure Democracy, by which I mean, a Society, consisting of a small number of citizens, who assemble and administer the Government in person, can admit of no cure for the mischiefs of faction. A common passion or interest will, in almost every case, be felt by a majority of the whole; a communication and concert results from the form of Government itself; and there is nothing to check the inducements to sacrifice the weaker party, or an obnoxious individual. Hence it is, that such Democracies have ever been spectacles of turbulence and contention; have ever been found incompatible with personal security, or the rights of property; and have in general been as short in their lives, as they have been violent in their deaths. Theoretic politicians, who have patronized this species of Government, have erroneously supposed, that by reducing mankind to a perfect equality in their political rights, they would, at the same time, be perfectly equalized and assimilated in their possessions, their opinions, and their passions.

A Republic, by which I mean a Government in which the scheme of representation takes place, opens a different prospect, and promises the cure for which we are seeking. Let us examine the points in which it varies from pure Democracy, and we shall comprehend both the nature of the cure, and the efficacy which it must derive from the Union.

The two great points of difference between a Democracy and a Republic are, first, the delegation of the Government, in the latter, to a small number of citizens elected by the rest: secondly, the greater number of citizens, and greater sphere of country, over which the latter may be extended.

The effect of the first difference is, on the one hand to refine and enlarge the public views, by passing them through the medium of a chosen body of citizens, whose wisdom may best discern the true interest of their country, and whose patriotism and love of justice, will be least likely to sacrifice it to temporary or partial considerations. Under

The Federalist, No. X. November 22, 1787. Library of Congress, Washington, D.C.

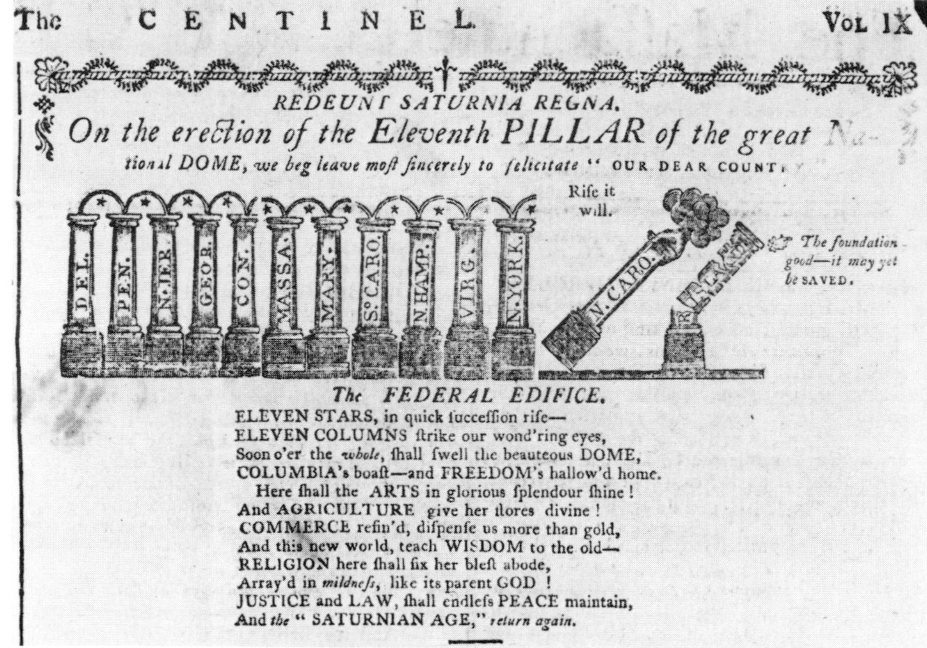

The CENTINEL. Vol IX

REDEUNT SATURNIA REGNA.

On the erection of the Eleventh PILLAR of the great National DOME, we beg leave most ſincerely to ſelicitate " OUR DEAR COUNTRY."

The FEDERAL EDIFICE.

ELEVEN STARS, in quick ſucceſſion riſe—
ELEVEN COLUMNS ſtrike our wond'ring eyes,
Soon o'er the *whole*, ſhall ſwell the beauteous DOME,
COLUMBIA's boaſt—and FREEDOM's hallow'd home.
Here ſhall the ARTS in glorious ſplendour ſhine!
And AGRICULTURE give her ſtores divine!
COMMERCE refin'd, diſpenſe us more than gold,
And this new world, teach WISDOM to the old—
RELIGION here ſhall fix her bleſt abode,
Array'd in *mildneſs*, like its parent GOD!
JUSTICE and LAW, ſhall endleſs PEACE maintain,
And *the* " SATURNIAN AGE," *return again.*

The last of eleven allegories in the *Massachusetts Centinel*, August 2, 1788, that traced the status of the Constitution's ratification. Library of Congress, Washington, D.C.

Patrick Henry was a powerful opponent of the Constitution because of its potential to weaken the states, and the threat he felt it posed to individual liberties. We hear echoes of those concerns in the most contemporary of constitutional debates.

Hamilton and John Jay worked mightily until a narrow victory was achieved in New York, despite the fact that the Antifederalists had originally outnumbered advocates of the Constitution in that state by a two-to-one margin. On March 4, 1789, the First Federal Congress under the Constitution convened; on April 30, George Washington was inaugurated as the first President. Finally, North Carolina and reluctant Rhode Island joined the other original states in ratifying the Constitution on November 21, 1789 and May 29, 1790, respectively, making the Union complete.

To establish a strong central government, the Constitution had to withdraw certain powers from the states and vest them in a national government. Even with a system of checks and balances, the Framers feared the possible consequences of concentrating power in this way. They therefore provided for representation of the states on an equal basis in the Senate, maintained state authority over internal commerce, and—through the amendment process—reserved certain powers to the states. The ensuing division of governmental authority between the states and the nation as a whole, known as federalism, has been a continuing source of constitutional debate ever since.

When the people of Hillsborough, New Hampshire won state support for their opposition to the establishment of a nuclear dump site in their community, the issue became one of states' rights. New Hampshire went on record: it did not want that nuclear dump in its territory. The federal government, however, has adopted policies promoting nuclear power. For nuclear power to remain viable, facilities must be established to dispose of its waste.

The problem of nuclear waste has intensified the debate over federal versus state interests. In the Midwest, a consortium of state officials has offered $40 million in economic benefits to any Indiana, Iowa, Michigan, Minnesota, Missouri, Ohio, or Wisconsin community that volunteers to be the site of a low-level radioactive waste facility. Low-level waste consists of contaminated materials such as gloves, clothing, or tools used at nuclear plants or in the practice of nuclear medicine. The materials decay to safe levels within one hundred years. However, the consortium has not found any volunteers despite the economic incentives promised.

While low-level nuclear waste is one problem, high-level waste, which remains radioactive for thousands of years, is what concerns the New Hampshire residents. In 1982, Congress passed the Nuclear Waste Policy Act in an attempt to find a solution to the problem. The Act required the Energy Department to open a western disposal site by 1998 and an eastern site shortly afterward. The Act gave states a veto over site selection, but also gave a majority in Congress the power to override that veto.

As is likely in New Hampshire—if it is selected as the site—the western candidates are not apt to welcome the disposal facility with open arms. When federal officials named a Texas county as one of three finalists for the western site in 1984, then-Governor Mark White said: "Before the people of Deaf Smith County glow in the dark, sparks will fly." Another possible site was equally negative—Washington voters passed a November 1986 state referendum opposing any waste facility in their state.

Second Bank of the United States, Philadelphia. In an early test case of federal supremacy over state law—*McCulloch* v. *Maryland* (1819)—Chief Justice John Marshall forcefully upheld national power. Still, the issue of a national bank that was part of the case continued to be debated, and when the charter of the Second Bank of the United States was renewed, President Andrew Jackson vetoed the congressional renewal on grounds of unconstitutionality. Independence National Historical Park, Philadelphia

If this stalemate continues, the federal government will be faced with the necessity of imposing the facility upon one western and one eastern state. It was this type of power that the Antifederalists most feared would be exercised by a central government against the wishes of the states. Yet it is precisely this type of federal power that, for example, overcame state opposition on civil rights matters. The Constitution's Framers never anticipated the scope of the possible conflict between state and national government, nor the development of shared responsibilities at the state and federal levels. To them, the majority of governmental functions remained the province of the states: crime and punishment, marriage, education, commercial law, and civil justice. The federal government was invested with certain specified powers that were thought unlikely to impinge upon the rights of individuals or states. As a further protection, the first ten amendments to the Constitution (the Bill of Rights) were added to protect individuals from the might of the federal government, as well as to protect the states. (The Tenth Amendment provides: "The powers not delegated to the United States by the Constitution, nor prohibited by it to the States, are reserved to the States respectively, or to the people.")

The burgeoning authority of the federal government in relation to the states became evident—although the issue was hardly settled—when the Supreme Court decided *McCulloch* v. *Maryland* (1819). Much of the political debate during the nation's early years was over a strict versus loose interpretation of the powers that the Constitution bestowed upon the federal government. When Congress proceeded to charter a national bank, relying on the Constitution's grant of all powers "necessary and proper," many thought their worst fears had been realized. The bank acted as any private bank would, except that it was also the depository of the United States government, which was treated as a preferred loan customer. The bank's charter expired in 1811, but a second Bank of the United States was established in 1816, despite fervent political opposition. It was a lightning rod for criticism right from the start, but added to the controversy surrounding its existence by issuing bad loans and engaging in speculation that contributed to the failure of several state-established banks.

Maryland was only one of several states that sought to impose taxes on the bank, in order to drive it out of the state. Kentucky, for example, had a much harsher tax of $60,000. Maryland imposed a two-percent tax on most bank notes, or an alternative annual tax of $15,000. The Maryland courts found that the statute had been violated and imposed penalties on James McCulloch, cashier of the Baltimore branch of the Bank of the United States.

The case was argued before the Supreme Court over a period of nine days. There were six counsel participating in the arguments, including Daniel Webster for the bank and Luther Martin (who had opposed a strong national government during the Constitutional Convention) for Maryland. Chief Justice John Marshall used the occasion to settle the debate over whether the states had established the federal government and thus its powers "must be exercised in subordination to the states, who alone possess supreme dominion." In rejecting the state supremacy position, Chief Justice Marshall wrote: "The government of the Union . . . is emphatically and truly a government of the people. In form and in substance it emanates from them, its powers are granted by them, and are to be exercised on them, and for their benefit."

McCulloch held that the federal government had the authority to address national problems. Chartering the second Bank of the United States, the Court said, was an appropriate means of regulating currency and resolving national economic problems. In addition, Maryland was found to be without authority to tax notes issued by the federal bank, because state legislation, including taxes, that interfered with valid federal powers comprised an unconstitutional interference with federal supremacy.

The year 1819 produced another case challenging state authority, but in a different context. *Trustees of Dartmouth College* v. *Woodward* involved a dispute over control between the college's governing board and the state of New Hampshire. The trustees argued that their royal charter was a contract protected from state interference by the Constitution. The state argued that no royal grant should be recognized in a democratic republic—but, even if the charter were valid, it was only a legislative act that could be changed by the New Hampshire legislature. The Supreme Court upheld the trustees and their contract theory as it was brilliantly argued by Daniel Webster.

A front View of DARTMOUTH COLLEGE, with the CHAPEL, & HALL.

Cricket on the Dartmouth Campus. 1793. In arguing emotionally—and successfully—for his alma mater, Dartmouth College, in *Trustees of Dartmouth College* v. *Woodward* (1819), Daniel Webster brought tears to the eyes of spectators and Justices alike. The Metropolitan Museum of Art, Bequest of Charles Allen Munn, 1924

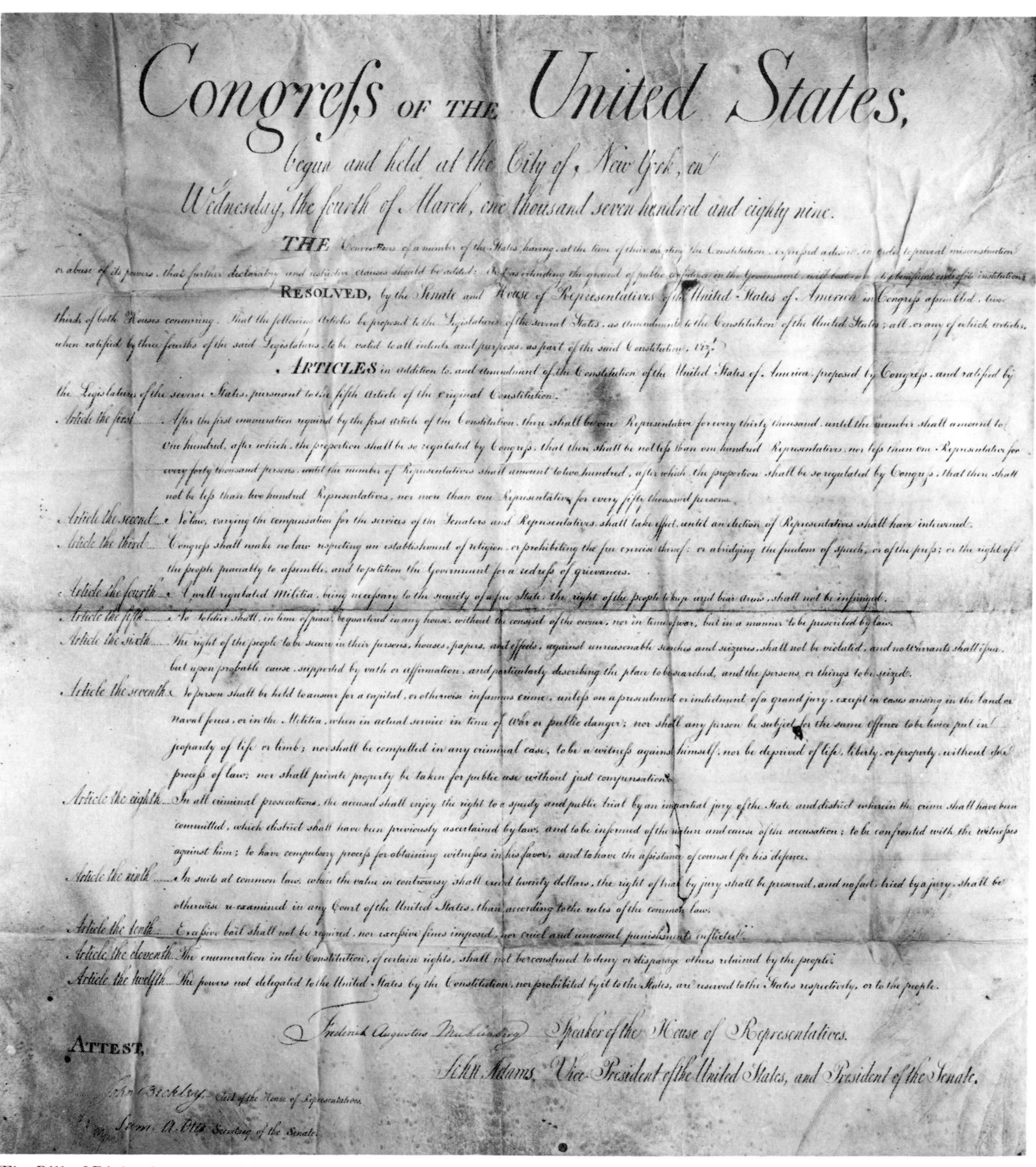

Congreſs of the United States,

begun and held at the City of New-York, on Wednesday, the fourth of March, one thousand seven hundred and eighty nine.

THE Conventions of a number of the States, having, at the time of their adopting the Constitution, expressed a desire, in order to prevent misconstruction or abuse of its powers, that further declaratory and restrictive clauses should be added: And as extending the ground of public confidence in the Government, will best ensure the beneficent ends of its institution.

RESOLVED, by the Senate and House of Representatives of the United States of America in Congress assembled, two thirds of both Houses concurring, that the following Articles be proposed to the Legislatures of the several States, as amendments to the Constitution of the United States, all, or any of which articles, when ratified by three fourths of the said Legislatures, to be valid to all intents and purposes, as part of the said Constitution; viz.

ARTICLES in addition to, and Amendment of the Constitution of the United States of America, proposed by Congress, and ratified by the Legislatures of the several States, pursuant to the fifth Article of the original Constitution.

Article the first... After the first enumeration required by the first article of the Constitution, there shall be one Representative for every thirty thousand, until the number shall amount to one hundred, after which, the proportion shall be so regulated by Congress, that there shall be not less than one hundred Representatives, nor less than one Representative for every forty thousand persons, until the number of Representatives shall amount to two hundred, after which the proportion shall be so regulated by Congress, that there shall not be less than two hundred Representatives, nor more than one Representative for every fifty thousand persons.

Article the second... No law, varying the compensation for the services of the Senators and Representatives, shall take effect, until an election of Representatives shall have intervened.

Article the third... Congress shall make no law respecting an establishment of religion, or prohibiting the free exercise thereof; or abridging the freedom of speech, or of the press; or the right of the people peaceably to assemble, and to petition the Government for a redress of grievances.

Article the fourth... A well regulated Militia, being necessary to the security of a free State, the right of the people to keep and bear Arms, shall not be infringed.

Article the fifth... No Soldier shall, in time of peace be quartered in any house, without the consent of the owner, nor in time of war, but in a manner to be prescribed by law.

Article the sixth... The right of the people to be secure in their persons, houses, papers, and effects, against unreasonable searches and seizures, shall not be violated, and no Warrants shall issue, but upon probable cause, supported by oath or affirmation, and particularly describing the place to be searched, and the persons or things to be seized.

Article the seventh... No person shall be held to answer for a capital, or otherwise infamous crime, unless on a presentment or indictment of a grand jury, except in cases arising in the land or naval forces, or in the Militia, when in actual service in time of War or public danger; nor shall any person be subject for the same offence to be twice put in jeopardy of life or limb; nor shall be compelled in any criminal case, to be a witness against himself, nor be deprived of life, liberty, or property, without due process of law; nor shall private property be taken for public use without just compensation.

Article the eighth... In all criminal prosecutions, the accused shall enjoy the right to a speedy and public trial by an impartial jury of the State and district wherein the crime shall have been committed, which district shall have been previously ascertained by law, and to be informed of the nature and cause of the accusation; to be confronted with the witnesses against him; to have compulsory process for obtaining witnesses in his favor, and to have the assistance of counsel for his defence.

Article the ninth... In suits at common law, where the value in controversy shall exceed twenty dollars, the right of trial by jury shall be preserved, and no fact, tried by a jury, shall be otherwise re-examined in any Court of the United States, than according to the rules of the common law.

Article the tenth... Excessive bail shall not be required, nor excessive fines imposed, nor cruel and unusual punishments inflicted.

Article the eleventh... The enumeration in the Constitution, of certain rights, shall not be construed to deny or disparage others retained by the people.

Article the twelfth... The powers not delegated to the United States by the Constitution, nor prohibited by it to the States, are reserved to the States respectively, or to the people.

Frederick Augustus Muhlenberg Speaker of the House of Representatives.

ATTEST,

John Adams, Vice-President of the United States, and President of the Senate.

John Beckley, Clerk of the House of Representatives.

Sam. A. Otis Secretary of the Senate.

The Bill of Rights began as a joint resolution proposing twelve amendments to the Constitution, which were submitted to the states for approval in 1789. Articles three through twelve were ratified in 1791 and became the first ten amendments, popularly known as the Bill of Rights. Library of Congress, Washington, D.C.

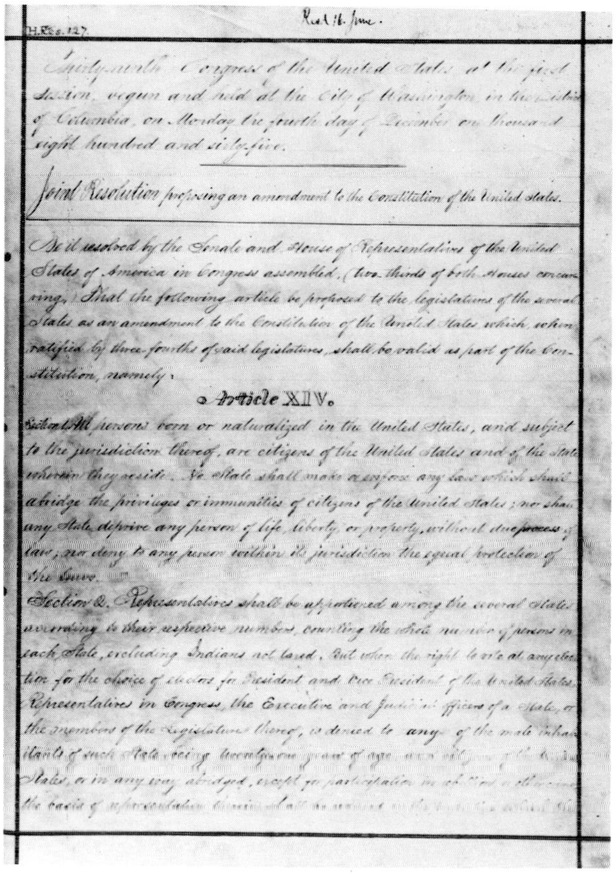

While *McCulloch* and *Woodward* might have made the future of the states appear bleak, it did not lead to the entire usurpation of power by the federal government that some feared. Even today, restrictions that prevent federal courts from rendering judgments based purely upon state law demonstrate how the Constitution still bars federal interference in matters of unqualified state concern. On the other hand, the Constitution remains the supreme law of the land, as exemplified by the fact that state constitutions and laws conflicting with the federal Constitution have been declared invalid time and time again. The passage of the Fourteenth Amendment vastly expanded that realm by "incorporating"—or applying to the states—many individual protections against government intrusions contained in the Bill of Rights. As a result, previously valid state laws were found to violate the Constitution's due process command. Earlier in this century, federal-state relations could be characterized as having been largely cooperative. With the growth of the federal bureaucracy, however, and the need for national solutions to many common problems,

First page of the Joint Resolution that became the Fourteenth Amendment to the Constitution. National Archives, Washington, D.C.

Chamber of the House of Representatives as President Franklin D. Roosevelt delivered his State of the Union address to a joint session of Congress on opening day of the third session of the seventy-sixth Congress. 1940. The Constitution separates the three branches of government, but they all come together for the constitutionally-mandated State of the Union address. Members of the Supreme Court are present, and listen attentively, but they do not applaud, because they may eventually be called upon to rule on the constitutionality of one of the President's proposals. AP/Wide World Photos

that relationship has become more heavily weighted on the side of nationally-imposed standards supported by grants-in-aid.

Today, federal regulatory authority has reached into nearly every aspect of public activity. Because of the Constitution's Supremacy Clause, states do not have any authority to legislate in a subject area that has been preempted by the federal government. The purpose of this principle is to avoid having conflicting rules emerge from different levels of government. Thus, if a state statute acts "as an obstacle to the accomplishment and execution of the full purposes and objectives of Congress," it will be considered superseded. Still, unique arrangements, such as the Clean Air Act, sometimes permit state regulations to further federal goals, but never to undercut them. Where no provisions are made for a state role, the states must rely on the political process to protect their interests.

The Constitution recognizes that states have political power. They are represented in Congress by a delegation whose members owe a certain loyalty to their home state. Joining with other states who face similar problems, they can wield considerable political clout. Congress, however, is but one actor in the federal system. Federal governmental power is dispersed through three branches: the legislative, the executive, and the judicial. In addition to distributing power between the states and the central government, the separation of powers within that central government was an attempt to mitigate the concern expressed by Lord Acton that "power tends to corrupt; and absolute power corrupts absolutely."

The system of separated powers the Framers established was a variation on a British theme. Their quarrel with the unwritten English constitutional system had more to do with the way it was practiced than with the ideal of balanced government it incorporated. Under the English system, the House of Lords and the House of Commons were powerful arms of the government that should have been able to keep the king in check. Influence-buying, however, corrupted the system.

Familiar with the doctrine advocated by Montesquieu, the Framers separated the legislative, executive, and judicial branches of government, but incorporated the English balanced government theory as well "to divide and arrange the several offices in such a manner as that each may be a check on the other," as Madison stated in *The Federalist* No. 51. To prevent the sort of corruption that was rampant in England, the Framers ensured the separation of powers by forbidding members of either house of Congress to hold office in the executive branch.

President Franklin D. Roosevelt's series of "fireside chats" heralded a new media age that enhanced the power of the presidency in the court of public opinion. This power has intensified with the pervasiveness of television. AP/Wide World Photos

Still, the system has not been without its tensions. By dividing governmental responsibilities between the President and the Congress, the Framers ensured that actions detrimental to the national interest could not be made in haste. However, they also set up a system that sometimes results in legislative-executive deadlock. The frustrations of that situation have led to alternating periods of executive and legislative dominance. Since the presidency of Franklin D. Roosevelt, there has been a tendency to fear the development of an "imperial presidency" because the holder of that office has the potential to provide national leadership in a manner that a divided Congress cannot. The President can speak with a single voice that has immediate access to the national press—and the attention of the nation—while Congress, made up of myriad members arguing among themselves and competing for attention, is an institution that has a built-in disadvantage in today's media-dominated age. Nevertheless, at the first sign of presidential weakness, Congress asserts itself and often prevails.

For example, when the Radical Republicans found Andrew Johnson too timid in establishing a Reconstruction program following the Civil War, they passed the Tenure-of-Office Act (later held unconstitutional), over a presidential veto. The Act was designed to prevent President Johnson from removing the Cabinet officers he had inherited from Abraham Lincoln. When he did seek to fire Secretary of War Edwin M. Stanton, impeachment proceedings were initiated. Johnson became the only President to be impeached, although he was spared conviction by a single vote.

The impeachment proceedings against President Andrew Johnson. 1868. The only President to be impeached thus far, Andrew Johnson escaped conviction by a single vote.

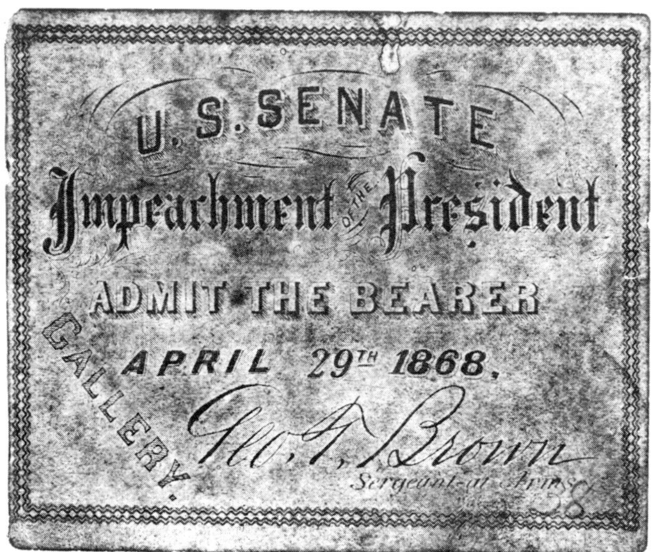

Admission to the Gallery of the U.S. Senate for the "Impeachment of the President." April 29, 1868. National Archives, Washington, D.C.

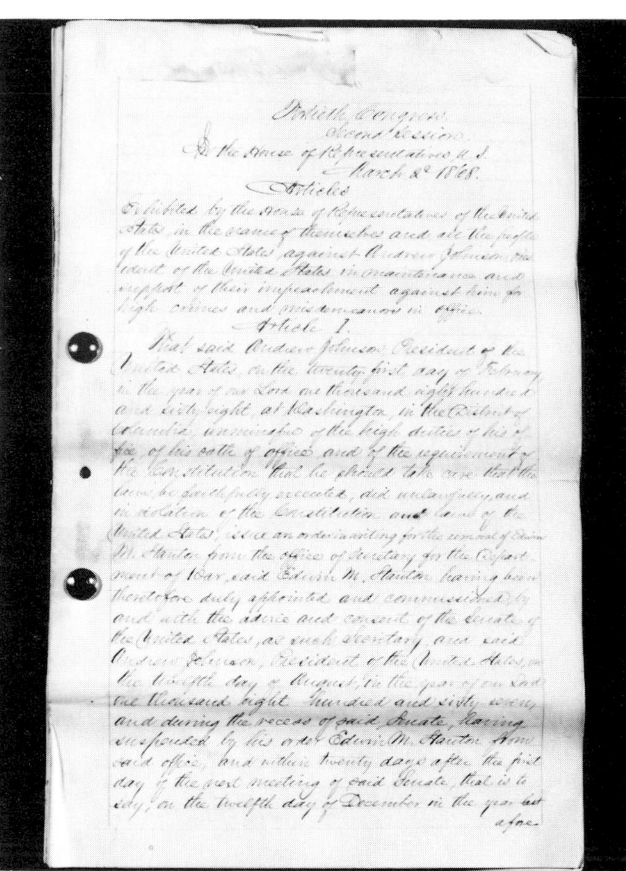

Fortieth Congress,
Second Session.
In the House of Representatives U.S.
March 2d 1868.

Articles

Exhibited by the House of Representatives of the United States, in the name of themselves and all the people of the United States, against Andrew Johnson, President of the United States, in maintenance and support of their impeachment against him for high crimes and misdemeanors in office.

Article I.

That said Andrew Johnson, President of the United States, on the twenty first day of February in the year of our Lord one thousand eight hundred and sixty eight, at Washington, in the District of Columbia, unmindful of the high duties of his office, of his oath of office, and of the requirement of the Constitution that he should take care that the laws be faithfully executed, did unlawfully, and in violation of the Constitution and laws of the United States, issue an order in writing for the removal of Edwin M. Stanton from the office of Secretary for the Department of War, said Edwin M. Stanton having been theretofore duly appointed and commissioned, by and with the advice and consent of the Senate of the United States, as such Secretary, and said Andrew Johnson, President of the United States, on the twelfth day of August, in the year of our Lord one thousand eight hundred and sixty seven, and during the recess of said Senate, having suspended by his order Edwin M. Stanton from said office, and within twenty days after the first day of the next meeting of said Senate, that is to say, on the twelfth day of December in the year last afore-

First page of the Articles of Impeachment brought against President Andrew Johnson. March 2, 1868. National Archives, Washington, D.C.

Caricature concerning "Mustering the Impeachment Managers." 1868. The New-York Historical Society

House of Representatives managers of the impeachment proceedings and trial of President Andrew Johnson. 1868. National Archives, Washington, D.C.

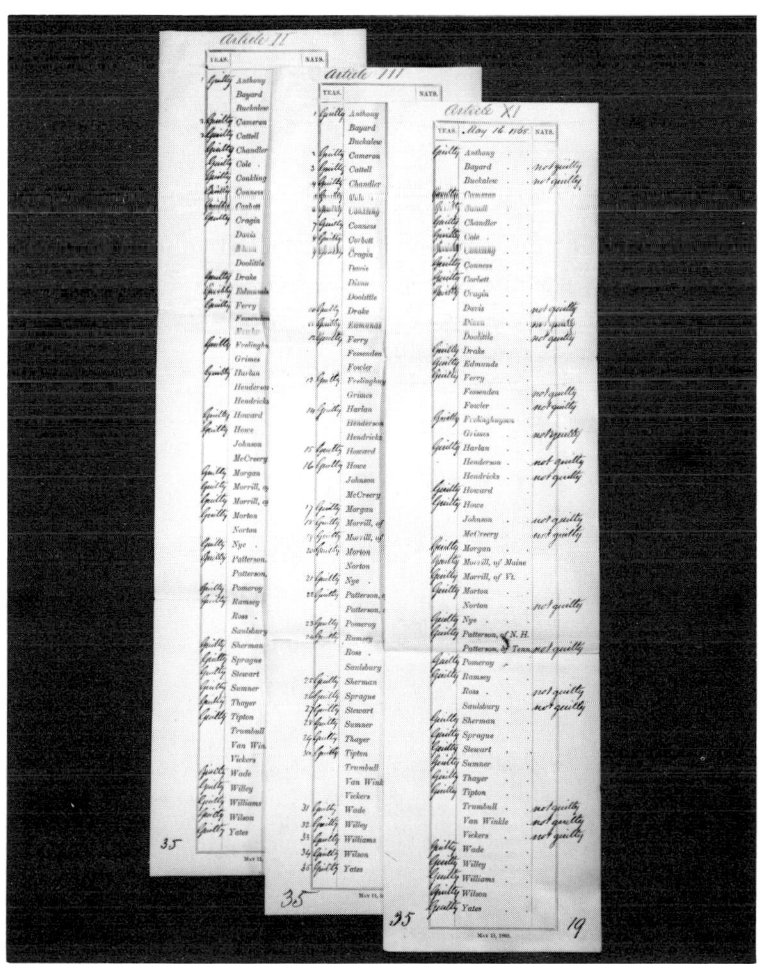

The vote as recorded on individual Articles of Impeachment brought against President Andrew Johnson. May 16, 1868. National Archives, Washington, D.C.

The Constitution provides for the removal of the President, Vice-President, or other federal officers "on Impeachment for, and Conviction of, Treason, Bribery, or other high Crimes and Misdemeanors." The House of Representatives is assigned responsibility for voting articles of impeachment, much as a grand jury presents an indictment. The individual impeached is then tried in the Senate. When the President is tried, the Chief Justice of the United States presides. A two-thirds vote in the Senate is necessary in order to convict and remove an impeached officer. In addition to Andrew Johnson, impeachment trials have involved a senator, a cabinet officer, a Supreme Court justice, and nine federal judges. Only five of these trials resulted in conviction and removal from office. Impeachment is difficult, even under the best of circumstances. In 1819, Thomas Jefferson complained: "It is a cumbersome, archaic process." It has not improved over the years.

This drawing shows U.S. District Judge John Sirica sentencing four former White House aides in the obstruction of justice case stemming from the Watergate break-in and cover-up. The aides are, from left to right, John Mitchell, John Ehrlichmann, H.R. Haldeman, and Robert Mardian. Washington, D.C. February 1975. AP/Wide World Photos

More than a century after Andrew Johnson, Richard Nixon eluded certain impeachment and likely conviction by resigning from office. The Watergate investigation, first carried forward by Congress and then by a special prosecutor, took center stage for the nation, as Congress seized its opportunity to take the initiative. Still, that body moved advisedly and cautiously, while the criminal cases proceeded. Seven members of the President's campaign and White House staffs were indicted for conspiracy to obstruct justice and certain other offenses related to a break-in at the headquarters of the opposition party. Richard Nixon himself was named by the grand jury as an "unindicted co-conspirator." The special prosecutor, Leon Jaworski, sought to subpoena certain White House tape recordings of specifically identified conversations between the President and his aides. With the White House resisting the subpoena, the Supreme Court agreed to hear the case on an expedited schedule.

When the Supreme Court rejected President Nixon's claim of executive privilege over apparently incriminating tape recordings—the "smoking gun" that prosecutors had sought—the drama moved to a rapid conclusion. On July 24, 1974, the same day the Supreme Court handed down the decision in *United States* v. *Nixon*, the House Judiciary Committee began its final public debate on the proposed articles of impeachment. During the next six days, the committee adopted three of those articles, charging obstruction of justice, abuse of presidential power, and unconstitutional defiance of House subpoenas. On August 9, 1974, Richard Nixon resigned from office.

Nowhere do the conflicts between the political branches have greater potential for collision than over the exercise of the

Members of the United States First Infantry Division coming under sniper fire in the field. Vietnam. 1966. AP/Wide World Photos

war powers. The power to wage war, particularly in the nuclear age, is perhaps the most awesome responsibility of government. The Constitution clearly assigns to Congress the power to declare war and raise revenues and armies for its engagement, but places the President at the head of the armed forces as Commander-in-Chief. It is significant that the Constitution provides for civilian control of the military, although how that authority is to be effectively shared by the governmental branches has never been settled satisfactorily. Indeed, in his *Eulogy on Madison* (1836), John Quincy Adams said: "The respective powers of the President and Congress of the United States, in the case of war with foreign powers are yet undetermined. Perhaps they can never be defined."

The Vietnam War was not the first or even the fifth of America's undeclared wars. From 1798 to 1800, the United States was engaged in an undeclared naval war with France over its interference with American shipping. In a case related to this action, Justice Bushrod Washington wrote: "Every contention by force, between two nations, in external matters, under the authority of their respective governments, is not only war, but public war." He recognized hostilities as being "more confined" than war and "limited to places, persons, and things." By recognizing something war-like that is less-than-war, the Court laid the groundwork for future disputes. Presidents traditionally seek greater leeway in conducting the na-

THE COPPERHEAD PARTY.—IN FAVOR OF *A VIGOROUS PROSECUTION OF PEACE!*

Northern cartoon of 1863 shows the Union threatened by political reptiles wearing the hats and collars of Midwest Democratic Congressmen. Culver Pictures

tional defense, while Congress is a sometimes reluctant partner in these military maneuvers.

The courts have been loath to interfere in the conduct of war. In the *Prize Cases* (1863), the Supreme Court held that President Abraham Lincoln was responding to an emergency in 1861 when he blockaded Southern ports three months before Congress approved the action. Justice Robert O. Grier wrote: "[However] long may have been its previous conception, [this civil war] nevertheless sprung forth suddenly from the parent brain, a Minerva in the full panoply of *war*. The President was bound to meet it in the shape it presented itself, without waiting for Congress to baptize it with a name; and no name given to it by him or them could change the fact."

Presidentially initiated military actions that lack congressional blessing have been justified on the basis of self-defense, treaty requirements, or protection of American interests. The third of these rationales served James Polk in 1845 as his justification for preventing Mexican interference in the annexation of Texas, and settling the new state's southern border; as well as being called upon by Theodore Roosevelt in 1903 when he sent troops to Panama—to support a revolution against Colombia and to secure the rights to build and operate a canal. In 1916, on similar grounds, Woodrow Wilson sent soldiers into Mexico after Pancho Villa, the bandit; and Harry Truman au-

Theodore Roosevelt as a Rough Rider. He was the first to assert that because the President is the only official elected by all the people, he has a special obligation to protect the public interest in times of crisis as he deems best—unless specifically forbidden by the Constitution. The Supreme Court has never agreed to this interpretation of the chief executive's authority. Courtesy Theodore Roosevelt Collection. Harvard College Library, Cambridge

thorized the 1950s "police action" in Korea under the same banner.

The Constitution's division of responsibilities has also been finessed in a number of informal ways. When Congress refused to appropriate funds for an around-the-world voyage by the navy as a show of military might, Theodore Roosevelt used funds already in the budget to send the fleet half-way around the world, and Congress had no choice but to appropriate the necessary funds to bring them back.

The Vietnam War brought a new focus to the war powers dilemma. Lyndon Johnson claimed authorization for that undeclared war as a result of the 1964 Gulf of Tonkin Resolution. The 1973 War Powers Act was an attempt by Congress to reassert its constitutional authority to control the commitment of military personnel in war-like hostilities, such as Vietnam. Passed over the veto of a Watergate-weakened Richard Nixon, the Act was called "the most unconstitutional measure Congress has ever passed," by Senator Barry Goldwater. Others, however, feel it fails to go far enough in redressing the modern imbalance between the presidency and the Congress in the conduct of military operations. The War Powers Act requires the President to consult with Congress before introducing military personnel into hostilities. It further requires the removal of troops after a sixty-to-ninety-day period, unless Congress

Steel workers in a union hall in Pittsburgh, Pennsylvania, gathered around a radio to hear that President Harry S Truman had ordered the Secretary of Commerce to seize the steel mills to avert a strike scheduled for April 9, 1952. AP/Wide World Photos

authorizes their continued presence. While its constitutionality has never been tested in the courts, the Act has been characterized by every President since its passage as an unconstitutional limitation on executive authority.

Although Presidents wield great power as "Commander-in-Chief," their power has remained subject to the checks and balances of the Constitution. During the Korean War, for example, steelworkers and their employers reached an impasse in contract negotiations. Federal agencies attempted to intervene to bring about a settlement, but without success. The workers called a strike for April 9, 1952.

President Truman was faced with a dilemma, since he believed a work stoppage would jeopardize the war effort. Although it could have resolved the wage dispute, he resisted an increase in steel prices because of rampant inflation. Several acts authorized national seizures for defense purposes, but they mandated slow and cumbersome procedures. The president also could have invoked the "cooling-off" provisions of the 1947 Taft-Hartley Act to delay the strike another eighty days, but he chose not to do so since he had opposed the Act when it was passed and invoking it would have antagonized his supporters among the labor unions. Instead, he simply ordered Commerce Secretary Charles Sawyer to seize most of the nation's steel mills and keep them running.

Continuing their operation under protest, the steel companies sued Sawyer, claiming that the seizure was not authorized by an act of Congress or by the Constitution. The case reached the Supreme Court where Justice Hugo L. Black, writing for a six-to-three majority, said: "The President's power, if any, to issue the order must stem either from an act of Congress or from the Constitution itself." Since no statute authorized a presidential seizure (in fact, Congress had rejected a provision in 1947 that would have permitted governmental seizures in times of emergency), the Court scrutinized the Constitution's grant of presidential power for authority and found it wanting. Black wrote: "Even though 'theater of war' be an expanding concept, we cannot with faithfulness to our constitutional system hold that the Commander-in-Chief of the Armed Forces has the ultimate power as such to take possession of private property in order to keep labor disputes from stopping production. This is a job for the Nation's lawmakers, not for its military authorities."

In that decision, *Youngstown Sheet & Tube Company* v. *Sawyer* (1952), Justice Black went on to say: "The Founders of this Nation entrusted the lawmaking power to the Congress alone in both good and bad times." It cannot be claimed by the President. Still, our constitutional system is a political arena in which every participant, from the President to the humblest citizen, has the potential to affect policy. This was part of the Constitution's design. Justice Robert H. Jackson explained this phenomenon in a concurring opinion in the steel seizure case: "While the Constitution diffuses power the better to secure liberty, it also contemplates that practice will integrate the dispersed powers into a workable government. It enjoins upon its branches separateness but interdependence, autonomy but reciprocity. Presidential powers are not fixed but fluctuate, depending upon their disjunction or conjunction with those of Congress."

Just as the President cannot invade the legislative sphere, the Congress cannot intrude upon the executive's prerogatives. Congress has enacted a panoply of legislation since 1932 with procedures that allow one or more of its houses or committees to review and veto the actions of a variety of administrative agencies. The majority of these acts were passed in the 1970s. The review provisions—known as legislative vetoes—have allowed Congress to delegate considerable regulatory authority to the President and the agencies under his control while, at the same time, retaining a check over the exercise of that authority. The constitutionality of the legislative veto came before the Supreme Court in an immigration case. Jagdish Rai Chadha, a Kenyan with a British passport who was born of Indian parents, applied for permanent resident status after his student visa expired. The request was granted by an

Harry S Truman by Greta Kempton. 1948 & 1970. National Portrait Gallery, Smithsonian Institution, Washington, D.C.

Aerial view of the United States Capitol. The Capitol sits on Pennsylvania Avenue some sixteen blocks from the White House. Even the design of Washington, D.C. reflects the separation the Constitution established between these two branches. UPI/Bettmann Newsphotos

immigration judge since Chadha was barred from returning to Kenya by reason of his British citizenship, and the United Kingdom would not accept him for at least a year.

In exercising a legislative veto function, the House of Representatives struck Chadha and five others from a list of 340 applicants for resident alien status. Chadha was ordered deported, but he challenged the constitutionality of the House action. In *INS* v. *Chadha* (1983), the Supreme Court held that, for Congress to exercise its legislative authority, the Constitution requires passage of a law, bill, or resolution by both houses and presentment to the President for his signature or possible veto. The one-house legislative veto exercised in this instance was thus found to be unconstitutional.

While arguments concerning presidential exercises of power and legislative vetoes can appear to be overly technical considerations, the separation of powers has, at its heart, the goal of preserving liberty. If we allow the technicalities to obscure this objective, the consequences could be dire, for procedures that frustrate popular action are often easily circumvented. The constitutional system has endured and prevailed, according to some, because it has provided for both stability and flexibility. The well-practiced procedures by which we make decisions concerning our joint future have been the source of much of that stability, as has our cultural adherence—more often than not—to constitutional values such as liberty, equality, and justice. These values were at the core of the development of our Constitution, and have been amplified because of respect for and faithfulness to the constitutional system.

That most reliable observer of the American political scene, whose words are as relevant today as they were when written a century and a half ago, Alexis de Tocqueville, observed: "If the lights that guide us ever go out, they will fade little by little, as if of their own accord. Confining ourselves to practice, we may lose sight of basic principles, and when these have been entirely forgotten we may apply the methods derived from them badly; we might be left without the capacity to invent new methods and only able to make a clumsy and an unintelligent use of wise procedures no longer understood."

It is our duty to try to keep those lights burning. Stating the ideals and basic outlines of a governmental system in a written document, such as the Constitution, may make the rule of law seem less vulnerable to the passage of time and the whims of individuals who temporarily occupy high office. Still, the Constitution does not, and cannot, contain all of the answers to questions of policy. It remains for the government it created, and the people themselves, to address those questions within the framework of the Constitution. After the Constitution was drafted, Thomas Jefferson observed: "We can no longer say there is nothing new under the sun. For this whole chapter of the history of man is new." It is a chapter that "We the People" must continue to write.

The Constitution of the United States on display in the National Archives Building. National Archives, Washington, D.C.

PART V

The Constitution— Past, Present, and Future

☆ ☆

Benjamin Franklin (1759) "They that can give up essential liberty to obtain a little temporary safety deserve neither liberty nor safety."

☆ ☆

George Mason (1776) ". . . no free government, or the blessings of liberty, can be preserved to any people, but by . . . a frequent recurrence to fundamental principles."

☆ ☆ ☆ ☆ ☆ ☆ ☆ ☆ ☆ ☆ ☆ ☆ ☆ ☆ ☆ ☆ ☆ ☆ ☆ ☆

Abigail Adams (1776) "... in the new code of laws which I suppose it will be necessary for you to make, I desire you would remember the ladies and be more generous and favourable to them than your ancestors.... If particular care and attention is not paid to the ladies, we are determined to foment a rebellion, and will not hold ourselves bound by any laws in which we have no voice or representation."

☆ ☆ ☆ ☆ ☆ ☆ ☆ ☆ ☆ ☆ ☆ ☆ ☆ ☆ ☆ ☆ ☆ ☆ ☆ ☆

Thomas Jefferson (1784) "Every government degenerates when trusted to the rulers of the people alone. The people themselves therefore are its only safe depositories."

☆ ☆ ☆ ☆ ☆ ☆ ☆ ☆ ☆ ☆ ☆ ☆ ☆ ☆ ☆ ☆ ☆ ☆ ☆ ☆

George Washington (1786) "No morn ever dawned more favorable than ours did; and no day was ever more clouded than the present! Wisdom and good examples are necessary at this time to rescue the political machine from the impending storm."

☆ ☆ ☆ ☆ ☆ ☆ ☆ ☆ ☆ ☆ ☆ ☆ ☆ ☆ ☆ ☆ ☆ ☆ ☆ ☆

John Adams (1787) "The deliberate union of so great and various a people in such a place is, without all partiality or prejudice, if not the greatest exertion of human understanding, the greatest single effort of national deliberation that the world has ever seen."

Alexander Hamilton (1787) "The subject speaks its own importance; comprehending in its consequences, nothing less than the existence of the UNION, the safety and welfare of the parts of which it is composed, the fate of an empire, in many respects, the most interesting in the world. It has been frequently remarked, that it seems to have been reserved to the people of this country, by their conduct and example, to decide the important question, whether societies of men are really capable or not, of establishing good government from reflection and choice, or whether they are forever destined to depend, for their political constitutions, on accident and force."

☆ ☆

George Washington (1787) ". . . some few things in the Constitution . . . which did not fully accord with my wishes, yet, having taken every circumstance seriously into consideration, I was convinced it approached nearer to perfection than any government hitherto instituted among men."

☆ ☆

John Jay (1787) "Nothing is more certain than the indispensable necessity of Government, and it is equally undeniable, that whenever and however it is instituted, the people must cede to it some of their natural rights, in order to vest it with requisite powers."

☆ ☆

Thomas Jefferson (1787) "The basis of our government being the opinion of the people, the very first object should be to keep that right; and were it left to me to decide whether we should have a government without newspapers, or newspapers without a government, I should not hesitate a moment to prefer the latter."

☆ ☆

James Wilson (1787) "[I]t will be found that there is given to the general government no power whatsoever concerning [the press]; and no law, in pursuance of the Constitution, can possibly be enacted to destroy that liberty."

☆ ☆

Alexander Hamilton (1787) "Laws are a dead letter without courts to expound and define their true meaning and operation."

☆ ☆

George Washington (1787) [Concerning the Framers of the Constitution] "I do not think we are more inspired, have more wisdom, or possess more virtue, than those who will come after us."

☆ ☆

Alexander Hamilton (1788) ". . . . The courts were designed to be an intermediate body between the people and the legislature, in order, among other things, to keep the latter within the limits assigned to their authority. The interpretation of the laws is the proper and peculiar province of the courts. A constitution is, in fact, and must be regarded by the judges as, a fundamental law. It therefore belongs to them to ascertain its meaning, as well as the meaning of any particular act proceeding from the legislative body. If there should happen to be an irreconcilable variance between the two, that which has the superior obligation and validity ought, of course, to be preferred, or, in other words, the Constitution ought to be preferred to the statute, the intention of the people to the intention of their agents. . . . "

☆ ☆

James Madison (1788) "It is of great importance in a republic not only to guard the society against the oppression of its rulers, but to guard one part of the society against the injustice of the other part. If men were angels, no government would be necessary."

☆ ☆

George Washington (1788) "It seems to me, then, little short of a miracle, that the Delegates from so many different States . . . different in their manners, circumstances, and prejudices should unite in forming a system of national Government."

☆ ☆

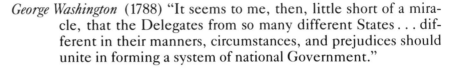

James Madison (1788) "A popular government without popular information, or the means of acquiring it, is but a prologue to a farce or a tragedy . . . and a people who mean to be their own governors must arm themselves with the power which knowledge gives."

☆ ☆

Benjamin Franklin (1789) "Our Constitution is in actual operation; everything appears to promise that it will last; but in this world nothing is certain but death and taxes."

☆ ☆

George Washington (1789) "I have always been persuaded that the stability and success of the National Government and consequently the happiness of the People of the United States, would depend in a considerable degree on the Interpretation and Execution of its Laws."

☆ ☆

Thomas Jefferson (1790) "The republican is the only form of government which is not eternally at open or secret war with the rights of mankind."

☆ ☆

Chief Justice John Jay (1790) "Let it be remembered that civil liberty consists not in a right to every man to do just what he pleases; but it consists in an equal right to all the citizens to have, enjoy, and do, in peace, security and without molestation, whatever the equal and constitutional laws of the country admit to be consistent with the public good."

☆ ☆

Alexander Hamilton (1791) "If the end be clearly comprehended within any of the specified powers, and if the measure have an obvious relation to that end, and is not forbidden by any particular provision of the Constitution, it may safely be deemed to come within the compass of the national authority."

☆ ☆

Thomas Jefferson (1799) "To the press alone, checquered as it is with abuses, the world is indebted for all the triumphs which have been gained by reason and humanity over error and oppression."

☆ ☆

Chief Justice John Marshall (1803) "Certainly all those who have framed written constitutions contemplate them as forming the fundamental and paramount law of the nation, and consequently, the theory of every such government must be, that an act of the legislature, repugnant to the constitution, is void. This theory is essentially attached to a written constitution, and is, consequently, to be considered, by this court, as one of the fundamental principles of our society."

Thomas Jefferson (1816) "Some men look at constitutions with sanctimonious reverence, and deem them like the ark of the covenant, too sacred to be touched. They ascribe to the men of the preceding age a wisdom more than human, and suppose what they did to be beyond amendment. I knew that age well; I belonged to it and labored with it. It deserved well of its country. . . . Laws and institutions must go hand in hand, with the progress of the human mind. As that becomes more developed, more enlightened, as new discoveries are made, new truths disclosed, and manners and opinions change with the change of circumstances, institutions must advance also, and keep pace with the times."

☆ ☆

Chief Justice John Marshall (1819) "A constitution, to contain an accurate detail of all the subdivisions of which its great powers will admit, and of all the means by which they may be carried into execution, would partake of the prolixity of a legal code, and could scarcely be embraced by the human mind. It would probably never be understood by the public. Its nature, therefore, requires that only its great outlines should be marked, its important objects designated, and the minor ingredients which compose those objects be deduced from the nature of the objects themselves. That this idea was entertained by the framers of the American Constitution, is not only to be inferred from the nature of the instrument, but from the language."

☆ ☆

Chief Justice John Marshall (1819) "Let the end be legitimate, let it be within the scope of the Constitution, and all means which are appropriate, which are plainly adapted to that end, which are not prohibited, but consist with the letter and spirit of the Constitution, are constitutional."

☆ ☆

Chief Justice John Marshall (1819) "That the power to tax involves the power to destroy; that the power to destroy may defeat and render useless the power to create; that there is a plain repugnance, in conferring on one government a power to control the constitutional measure of another, which other, with respect to those very measures, is declared to be supreme over that which exerts the control, are propositions not to be denied."

☆ ☆

Chief Justice John Marshall (1824) "The federal commerce power reaches all commerce which concerns more than one state. Once a subject is found to be interstate commerce or foreign trade, the power of Congress to regulate it is complete in itself, may be exercised to its ultimate extent, and acknowledges no limitations other than are prescribed in the Constitution."

Daniel Webster (1830) "It is, Sir, the people's Constitution, the people's government, made for the people, made by the people, and answerable to the people. That other sentiment, dear to every true American heart—Liberty and Union, now and forever, one and inseparable."

Andrew Jackson (1832) "The Constitution is still the object of our reverence, the bond of our Union, our defense in danger, the source of our prosperity in peace. It shall descend, as we have received it, uncorrupted by sophistical construction, to our posterity; and the sacrifices of local interest, of State prejudices, of personal animosities that were made to bring it into existence, will again be patriotically offered for its support."

James Madison (1835) "Whatever may be the judgment pronounced on the competency of the architects of the Constitution, or whatever may be the destiny of the edifice prepared by them, I feel it a duty to express my profound and solemn conviction . . . that there never was an assembly of men, charged with a great and arduous trust, who were more pure in their motives, or more exclusively or anxiously devoted to the object committed to them."

Alexis de Tocqueville (1835) "Within these limits the power vested in the American courts of justice of pronouncing a statute to be unconstitutional forms one of the most powerful barriers that have ever been devised against the tyranny of political assemblies."

☆ ☆

Chief Justice Roger B. Taney (1837) "The object and the end of all government is to promote the happiness and prosperity of the community by which it is established, and it can never be assumed that the government intended to diminish its power of accomplishing the end for which it was created. . . . While the rights of private property are sacredly guarded, we must not forget that the community also have rights, and the happiness and well being of every citizen depends on their faithful preservation."

☆ ☆

John Quincy Adams (1839) "The Declaration of Independence and the Constitution of the United States are part of one consistent whole, founded upon one and the same theory of government."

☆ ☆

Henry Clay (1850) "The Constitution of the United States was made not merely for the generation that then existed, but for posterity—unlimited, undefined, endless, perpetual posterity."

☆ ☆

Abraham Lincoln (1858) "I believe this government cannot endure, permanently half slave and half free."

☆ ☆

Abraham Lincoln (1861) "If by the mere force of numbers a majority should deprive a minority of any clearly written constitutional right, it might, in a moral point of view, justify revolution—certainly would if such a right were a vital one. . . . This country, with its institutions, belongs to the people who inhabit it. Whenever they shall grow weary of the existing government, they can exercise their constitutional right of amending it, or their revolutionary right to dismember or overthrow it."

Abraham Lincoln (1863) "The world will little note nor long remember what we say here, but it can never forget what they did here. It is for us, the living, rather to be dedicated here to the unfinished work which they who fought here have thus far so nobly advanced. It is rather for us to be here dedicated to the great task remaining before us—that from these honored dead we take increased devotion; that we here highly resolve that these dead shall not have died in vain; that this nation shall have a new birth of freedom; and that government of the people, by the people, for the people, shall not perish from the earth."

☆ ☆

Justice David Davis (1866) "The Constitution of the United States is a law for rulers and people, equally in war and in peace, and covers with the shield of its protection all classes of men, at all times, and under all circumstances. No doctrine involving more pernicious consequences was ever invented by the wit of man than that any of its provisions can be suspended during any of the great exigencies of government. Such a doctrine leads directly to anarchy or despotism."

☆ ☆

Andrew Johnson (1867) "Whenever administration fails or seems to fail in securing any of the great ends for which republican government is established, the proper course seems to be to renew the original spirit and forms of the Constitution itself."

☆ ☆

Susan B. Anthony (1873) "It was we, the people; not we, the white male citizens; nor yet we, the male citizens; but we, the whole people, who formed the Union. For any state to make sex a qualification that must ever result in disenfranchisement of an entire half of the people is to pass a bill of attainder, or an *ex post facto* law, and is therefore in violation of the supreme law of the land."

☆ ☆

Chief Justice Morrison R. Waite (1877) "An owner who devotes his property to a use in which the public has an interest . . . in effect grants the public an interest in that use, and must submit to be controlled by the public for the common good; to the extent of the interest he has thus created."

☆ ☆

Justice John Marshall Harlan (1883) "There cannot be in this republic any class of human beings in practical subjection to another class."

☆ ☆

William Gladstone (1887) "I have always regarded that Constitution as the most remarkable work known to me in modern times to have been produced by the human intellect, at a single stroke (so to speak), in its application to political affairs."

☆ ☆

Justice John Marshall Harlan (1887) "The courts are not bound by mere forms, nor are they to be misled by mere pretenses. They are at liberty—indeed, are under a solemn duty—to look at the substance of things, whenever they enter upon the inquiry whether the legislature has transcended the limits of its authority. If, therefore, a statute purporting to have been enacted to protect the public health, the public morals, or the public safety, has no real or substantial relation to those objects, or is a palpable invasion of rights secured by the fundamental law, it is the duty of the courts to so adjudge, and thereby give effect to the Constitution."

☆ ☆

Justice John Marshall Harlan (1896) "The arbitrary separation of citizens, on the basis of race, while they are on a public highway, is a badge of servitude wholly inconsistent with the civil freedom and the equality before the law established by the Constitution. . . . [We] boast of the freedom enjoyed by our people above all other peoples. But it is difficult to reconcile the boast with a state of the law which, practically, puts the brand of servitude and degradation upon a large class of our fellow citizens—our equals before the law. The thin disguise of 'equal' accommodations for passengers in railroad coaches will not mislead anyone, nor atone for the wrong this day done."

☆ ☆

Justice John Marshall Harlan (1896) "In the view of the Constitution, in the eye of the law, there is in this country no superior, dominant, ruling class of citizens. There is no caste here. Our Constitution is color-blind, and neither knows nor tolerates classes among citizens. In respect of civil rights, all citizens are equal before the law. The humblest is the peer of the most powerful."

☆ ☆

Justice Oliver Wendell Holmes, Jr. (1905) "A Constitution is not intended to embody a particular economic theory."

☆ ☆

Justice Charles Evans Hughes (1907) "We are under a Constitution, but the Constitution is what the judges say it is, and the judiciary is the safeguard of our liberty and of our property under the Constitution."

☆ ☆

Justice Oliver Wendell Holmes, Jr. (1913) "Let me turn to . . . that other visible court to which for 10 now accomplished years it has been my opportunity to belong. We are very quiet there, but it is the quiet of a storm center, as we all know. Science has taught the world scepticism, and has made it legitimate to put everything to the test of proof. Many beautiful and noble reverences are impaired, but in these days no one can complain if any institution, system, or belief is called on to justify its continuance in life. Of course we are not excepted and have not escaped. Doubts are expressed that go to our very being. Not only are we told that when Marshall pronounced an act of Congress unconstitutional he usurped a power that the Constitution did not give, but we are told that we are the representatives of a class—a tool of the money power. I get letters, not always anonymous, intimating that we are corrupt. Well, gentlemen, I admit that it makes my heart ache. It is very painful, when one spends all the energies of one's soul in trying to do good work, with no thought but that of solving a problem according to the rules by which one is bound, to know that many see sinister motives and would be glad of evidence that one was consciously bad. But we must take such things philosophically and try to see what we can learn from hatred and distrust, and whether behind them there may not be some germ of inarticulate truth.

.... As law embodies beliefs that have triumphed in the battle of ideas and then have translated themselves into action; while there still is doubt, while opposite convictions still keep a battle front against each other, the time for law has not come; the notion destined to prevail is not yet entitled to the field. It is a misfortune if a judge reads his conscious or unconscious sympathy with one side or the other prematurely into the law, and forgets that what seem to him to be first principles are believed by half his fellow men to be wrong.

.... For most of the things that properly can be called evils in the present state of the law I think the main remedy, as for the evils of public opinion, is for us to grow more civilized."

☆ ☆

Justice Oliver Wendell Holmes, Jr. (1918) ".... When men have realized that time has upset many fighting faiths, they may come to believe even more than they believe the very foundations of their own conduct that the ultimate good desired is better reached by free trade in ideas—that the best test of truth is the power of the thought to get itself accepted in the competition of the market, and that truth is the only ground upon which their wishes safely can be carried out. That at any rate is the theory of our Constitution. It is an experiment, as all life is an experiment. Every year if not every day we have to wager our salvation upon some prophecy based upon imperfect knowledge. ... Only the emergency that makes it immediately dangerous to leave the correction of evil counsels to time warrants making any exception to the sweeping command, 'Congress shall make no law ... abridging the freedom of speech.' "

☆ ☆

Justice Oliver Wendell Holmes, Jr. (1919) "The most stringent protection of free speech would not protect a man in falsely shouting fire in a theater and causing a panic. . . . The question in every case is whether the words used are used in such circumstances and are of such a nature as to create a clear and present danger that they will bring about the substantive evils that Congress has a right to prevent."

☆ ☆

Clarence Darrow (1920) "You can only protect your liberties in this world by protecting the other man's freedom. You can only be free if I am free."

☆ ☆

Chief Justice William Howard Taft (1921) "The Constitution was intended, its very purpose was, to prevent experimentation with the fundamental rights of the individual."

☆ ☆

Justice Louis D. Brandeis (1927) "Those who won our independence believed that the final end of the State was to make men free to develop their faculties; and that in its government the deliberative forces should prevail over the arbitrary. They valued liberty both as an end and as a means. They believed liberty to be the secret of happiness and courage to be the secret of liberty. They believed that freedom to think as you will and to speak as you think are means indispensable to the discovery and spread of political truth; that without free speech and assembly discussion would be futile; that with them, discussion affords ordinarily adequate protection against the dissemination of noxious doctrine; that the greatest menace to freedom is an inert people; that public discussion is a political duty; and that this should be a fundamental principle of the American government. They recognized the risks to which all human institutions are subject. But they knew that order cannot be secured merely through fear of punishment for its infraction; that it is hazardous to discourage thought, hope, and imagination; that fear breeds repression; that repression breeds hate; that hate menaces stable government; that the path of safety lies in the opportunity to discuss freely supposed grievances and proposed remedies; and that the fitting remedy for evil counsels is good ones. Believing in the power of reason as applied through public discussion, they eschewed silence coerced by law—the argument of force in its worst form. Recognizing the occasional tyrannies of governing majorities, they amended the Constitution so that free speech and assembly should be guaranteed.

Fear of serious injury cannot alone justify suppression of free speech and assembly. Men feared witches and burned women. It is the function of speech to free men from the bondage of irrational fears. To justify suppression of free speech there must be reasonable ground to fear that serious evil will result if free speech is practiced. There must be reasonable ground to believe that the evil to be prevented is imminent. There must be reasonable ground to believe that the evil to be prevented is a serious one. . . .

Those who won our independence by revolution were not cowards. They did not fear political change. They did not exalt order at the cost of liberty. To courageous, self-reliant men, with confidence in the power of free and fearless reasoning applied through the processes of popular government, no danger flowing from speech can be deemed clear and present, unless the incidence of the evil apprehended is so imminent that it may befall before there is opportunity for full discussion. If there be time to expose through discussion the falsehood and fallacies, to avert the evil by the processes of education, the remedy to be applied is more speech, not enforced silence. Only an emergency can justify repression. Such must be the rule if authority is to be reconciled with freedom. Such, in my opinion, is the command of the Constitution. It is therefore always open to Americans to challenge a law abridging free speech and assembly by showing that there was no emergency justifying it."

☆ ☆

Justice Louis D. Brandeis (1928) "The makers of our Constitution sought to protect Americans. . . . They conferred, as against the government, the right to be left alone—the most comprehensive of rights and the right most valued by civilized men."

Justice Louis D. Brandeis (1928) "The greatest dangers to liberty lurk in insidious encroachment by men of zeal, well-meaning but without understanding."

☆ ☆

Chief Justice Charles Evans Hughes (1930) "Dissent in a court of last resort is an appeal to the brooding spirit of law, to the intelligence of a future day, when a later decision may possibly correct the error into which the dissenting judge believes the court to have been betrayed."

☆ ☆

Justice Louis D. Brandeis (1932) ". . . in cases involving the Federal Constitution, where correction through legislative action is practically impossible, this Court has often overruled its earlier decisions. The Court bows to the lessons of experience and the force of better reasoning, recognizing that the process of trial and error, so fruitful in the physical sciences, is appropriate also in the judicial function."

☆ ☆

Justice George Sutherland (1932) "Even the intelligent and educated layman has small and sometimes no skill in the science of the law. . . . He requires the guiding hand of counsel at every step in the proceedings against him. Without it, though he be not guilty, he faces the danger of conviction because he does not know how to establish his innocence."

☆ ☆

Justice Owen J. Roberts (1934) "The Constitution does not secure to anyone liberty to conduct his business in such fashion as to inflict injury upon the public at large, or upon any substantial group of people."

☆ ☆

Justice James R. McReynolds (1935) "Plainly, I think, this Court must have regard to the wisdom of the enactment. At least, we must inquire concerning its purpose and decide whether the means proposed have reasonable relation to something within legislative power—whether the end is legitimate, and the means appropriate."

☆ ☆

Justice Harlan Fiske Stone (1935) "It is a contradiction in terms to say that there is power to spend for the national welfare, while rejecting any power to impose conditions reasonably adapted to the attainment of the end which alone would justify the expenditure."

☆ ☆

Justice Benjamin Cardozo (1937) "Freedom of speech and assembly comprise the very essence of a scheme of ordered liberty . . . the matrix, the indispensable condition of nearly every other form of freedom."

☆ ☆ ☆ ☆ ☆ ☆ ☆ ☆ ☆ ☆ ☆ ☆ ☆ ☆ ☆ ☆ ☆ ☆ ☆ ☆

Evans Hughes (1937) "What is this freedom? [i.e.,
ected by the due process clauses of the Fifth
ndments] The liberty safeguarded is lib-
on which requires the protection of
menace the health, safety, mor-
The exploitation of a class of
with respect to bargain-
against the denial
health and well
upon the
what is in
he commu-
abuse which
interest."

☆ ☆ ☆ ☆ ☆ ☆ ☆

d to a world founded upon
e first is freedom of speech
he world. The second is free-
God in his own way—every-
rd is freedom from want. The

Garrison - Abolitionist
Harriet Beech Stowe -
Dredd Scott - Case
Missouri Compro 1820
Scott 1 Remained slave in Missouri - 6 yrs litigation
Scott vs Sanford - still a slave 1860
13th Amend - 1865 - Abolish slavery.
14th Amend - Due Process Equal.

☆ ☆

Justice Robert H. Jackson (1943) "The very purpose of a Bill of Rights was to withdraw certain subjects from the vicissitudes of political controversy, to place them beyond the reach of majorities and officials and to establish them as legal principles to be applied by the courts. . . . If there is any fixed star in our constitutional constellation, it is that no official, high or petty, can prescribe what shall be orthodox in politics, nationalism, religion or other matters of opinion or force citizens to confess by word or act their faith therein. If there be any circumstances which permit an exception, they do not now occur to us."

☆ ☆

Justice Hugo L. Black (1947) "The establishment of religion clause of the First Amendment means at least this: Neither a state nor the Federal Government can set up a church. Neither can pass laws which aid one religion, aid all religions, or prefer one religion over another. The First Amendment has erected a wall between church and state. That wall must be kept high and impregnable. We could not approve the slightest breach."

☆ ☆

Justice Robert H. Jackson (1949) "There is danger that, if the Court does not temper its doctrinaire logic with a little practical wisdom, it will convert the constitutional Bill of Rights into a suicide pact."

☆ ☆

Justice Felix Frankfurter (1951) "Freedom of expression is the well-spring of our civilization. . . . The history of civilization is in considerable measure the displacement of error which once held sway as official truth by beliefs which in turn have yielded to other truths. Therefore the liberty of man to search for truth ought not to be fettered, no matter what orthodoxies he may challenge. Liberty of thought soon shrivels without freedom of expression. Nor can truth be pursued in an atmosphere hostile to the endeavor or under dangers which are hazarded only by heroes."

☆ ☆

Chief Justice Earl Warren (1954) "We conclude that in the field of public education the doctrine of 'separate but equal' has no place. Separate educational facilities are inherently unequal. . . ."

☆ ☆

Harry S Truman (1955) "I have little patience with people who take the Bill of Rights for granted. The Bill of Rights, contained in the first ten amendments to the Constitution, is every American's guarantee of freedom."

☆ ☆

Harry S Truman (1955) "If there is one basic element in our Constitution, it is civilian control of the military."

☆ ☆

Justice Hugo L. Black (1960) "The Framers knew that free speech is the friend of change and revolution. But they also knew that it is always the deadliest enemy of tyranny."

☆ ☆

J. William Fulbright (1964) "We are inclined to confuse freedom and democracy, which we regard as moral principles, with the way in which these are practiced in America—with capitalism, federalism and the two-party system, which are not moral principles, but simply the accepted practices of the American people."

☆ ☆

Justice William J. Brennan, Jr. (1964) "We consider this case [*New York Times Co.* v. *Sullivan*] against the background of a profound national commitment to the principle that debate on public issues should be uninhibited, robust, and wide-open, and that it may well include vehement, caustic, and sometimes unpleasantly sharp attacks on government and public officials."

☆ ☆

Chief Justice Earl Warren (1964) "Legislators represent people, not trees or acres. Legislators are elected by voters, not farms or cities or economic interests. As long as ours is a representative form of government, and our legislatures are those instruments of government elected directly by and directly representative of the people, the right to elect legislators in a free and unimpaired fashion is a bedrock of our political system. . . .

. . . . The fact that an individual lives here or there is not a legitimate reason for overweighting or diluting the efficacy of his vote. The complexions of societies and civilizations change, often with amazing rapidity. A nation once primarily rural in character becomes predominantly urban. Representation schemes once fair and equitable become archaic and outdated. But the basic principle of representative government remains, and must remain, unchanged—the weight of a citizen's vote cannot be made to depend on where he lives. Population is, of necessity, the starting point for consideration and the controlling criterion for judgment in legislative apportionment controversies. A citizen, qualified voter, is not more nor less so because he lives in the city or on the farm. This is the clear and strong command of our Constitution's Equal Protection Clause. This is an essential part of the concept of a government of laws and not men. . . . "

☆ ☆

Chief Justice Earl Warren (1966) "The prosecution may not use statements, whether exculpatory or inculpatory, stemming from custodial interrogation of the defendant unless it demonstrates the use of procedural safeguards effective to secure the privilege against self-incrimination. By custodial interrogation, we mean questioning by law enforcement officers after a person has been taken into custody or otherwise deprived of his freedom of action in any significant way. . . . Prior to any questioning, the person must be warned that he has a right to remain silent, that any statement he does make may be used as evidence against him, and that he has a right to the presence of an attorney, either retained or appointed. The defendant may waive effectuation of these rights, provided the waiver is made voluntarily, knowingly and intelligently. If, however, he indicates in any manner and at any stage of the process, that he wishes to consult with an attorney before speaking there can be no questioning. Likewise, if the individual is alone and indicates in any manner that he does not wish to be interrogated, the police may not question him. . . . "

☆ ☆

Justice Lewis F. Powell, Jr. (1972) "The price of lawful dissent must not be a dread of subjection to an unchecked surveillance power. Nor must the fear of unauthorized official eavesdropping deter vigorous citizen dissent and discussion of government action in private conversation. . . . We cannot accept the government's argument that internal security matters are too subtle and complex for judicial evaluation. . . . If the threat is too subtle or complex for our senior law enforcement officers to convey its significance to a court, one may question whether there is probable cause for surveillance."

☆ ☆

Justice William O. Douglas (1972) "The function of the press is to explore and investigate events, inform the people what is going on, and to expose the harmful as well as the good influences at work. There is no higher function performed under our constitutional regime."

☆ ☆

Chief Justice Warren E. Burger (1974) "We therefore reaffirm that it is 'emphatically the province and duty' of this court 'to say what the law is' with respect to the claim of privilege in this case. . . . [*United States* v. *Richard M. Nixon*]

The President's need for complete candor and objectivity from advisers calls for great deference from the courts. However, when the privilege depends solely on the broad undifferentiated claim of public interest in the confidentiality of such conversations, a confrontation with other values arises. Absent a claim of need to protect military, diplomatic or sensitive national security secrets, we find it difficult to accept the argument that even the very important interest in confidentiality of Presidential communications is significantly diminished by production of such material for *in camera* inspection. . . .

The very integrity of the judicial system and public confidence in the system depend on full disclosure of all the facts, within the framework of the rules of evidence. . . .

When the ground for asserting privilege as to subpoenaed materials for use in a criminal trial is based only on the generalized interest in confidentiality, it cannot prevail over the fundamental demands of due process of law in the fair administration of criminal justice. The generalized assertion of privilege must yield to the demonstrated specific need for evidence in a pending criminal trial."

☆ ☆

Chief Justice Warren E. Burger (1983) "To maintain the separation of powers, designed to prevent improvident exercise of power, the carefully defined limits on the power of each Branch must not be eroded. . . . With all the obvious flaws of delay, untidiness, and potential for abuse . . . we have not yet found a better way to preserve freedom than by making the exercise of power subject to the carefully crafted restraints spelled out in the Constitution."

Justice William J. Brennan, Jr. (1986) ". . . . This Court is final on constitutional matters. Outside of overruling itself, only constitutional amendments can change the constitutional interpretations that the Court renders, and because of that fact, I have always felt that a member of this Court is duty-bound to continue stating the constitutional principles that have governed his decisions, even if they are in dissent, against the day when they may no longer be in dissent. It has happened so often in the history of the Court, and must continue to happen, that views that represent the minority position come to be understood as correct. . . . "

Bibliography

American Bar Foundation. *Sources of Our Liberties*. Chicago: ABA Press, 1978. Text of major governing documents and declarations of rights such as Magna Carta and U.S. Constitution, with introductory essays.

Berger, Raoul. *Government by Judiciary: The Transformation of the Fourteenth Amendment*. Cambridge: Harvard University Press, 1977. An historical examination of the uses and abuses of judicial power by an advocate of restraint.

Bickel, Alexander M. *The Least Dangerous Branch: The Supreme Court at the Bar of Politics*. New Haven: Yale University Press, 1986, reprint. The unique role of the Supreme Court in the American democracy, from *Marbury* v. *Madison* to *Brown* v. *Board of Education*, is examined.

Bowen, Catherine Drinker. *Miracle at Philadelphia: The Story of the Constitutional Convention, May to September 1787*. Boston: Little, Brown & Co., 1966. A reliable account, dramatically told, of the Constitutional Convention.

Friendly, Fred W. *Minnesota Rag: The Dramatic Story of the Landmark Case that Gave New Meaning to Freedom of the Press*. New York: Random House, 1982. The story of the 1931 decision in *Near* v. *Minnesota*.

Garraty, John A., ed. *Quarrels That Have Shaped the Constitution*. New York: Harper & Row, 1964. Essays, originally published in *American Heritage*, on important Supreme Court cases.

Hamilton, Alexander, James Madison and John Jay. *The Federalist Papers*. New York: Bantam, 1961. A collection of essays written to help win ratification of the Constitution.

Kammen, Michael. *A Machine That Would Go of Itself: The Constitution in American Culture*. New York: Alfred A. Knopf, 1986. How American perceptions of the Constitution—often wrong—have helped make constitutional history.

Kluger, Richard. *Simple Justice: The History of Brown v. Board of Education and Black America's Struggle for Equality*. New

York: Alfred A. Knopf, 1977. The story of the battle against segregated schools from the Reconstruction era to the modern civil rights movement.

Levy, Leonard W. *Emergence of a Free Press*. New York: Oxford University Press, 1985. The origins of the American concept of a free press and its early years after the passage of the First Amendment.

Lewis, Anthony. *Gideon's Trumpet*. New York: Random House, 1964. The story of the 1962 decision in *Gideon* v. *Wainwright*, establishing the right of indigent defendants to free legal representation in felony cases.

Murphy, Paul L. *The Constitution in Crisis Times, 1918–1969*. New York: Harper & Row, 1972. An historical examination of the development of civil liberties and civil rights

O'Brien, David M. *Storm Center: The Supreme Court in American Politics*. New York: W. W. Norton, 1986. An account, rich with historical footnotes, of how the Supreme Court works.

Peck, Robert S. and Ralph S. Pollock, eds. *The Blessing of Liberty: Bicentennial Lectures at the National Archives*. Chicago: ABA Press, 1986. Essays by prominent scholars on a wide range of constitutional topics.

Schwartz, Bernard. *The Great Rights of Mankind: A History of the American Bill of Rights*. New York: Oxford University Press, 1977. A basic history of American civil liberties.

Shnayerson, Robert. *The Illustrated History of the Supreme Court of the United States*. New York: Harry N. Abrams, Inc., 1986. Text and images combine to show how the Court functions, and then to trace the development of the judicial branch from its earliest days into a fully coequal force in the government of the United States of America.

Stearns, Jean. *The Federalist Without Tears*. Washington, D.C.: University Press of America, 1977. *The Federalist Papers* translated into modern language.

Index

Pages on which illustrations appear are in *italics*.

Photo Credits—Part V

Benjamin Franklin, detail (National Portrait Gallery, Smithsonian Institution, Washington, D.C.); George Mason (Virginia State Library, Richmond); Abigail Adams (Boston Athenaeum Library); Thomas Jefferson (Maryland Historical Society); George Washington (The New-York Historical Society); John Adams, detail (National Portrait Gallery, Smithsonian Institution, Washington, D.C.); Alexander Hamilton (National Gallery of Art, Smithsonian Institution, Washington, D.C., Gift of the Avalon Foundation, 1952); George Washington (The New-York Historical Society); John Jay (The New-York Historical Society); Thomas Jefferson (Maryland Historical Society); James Wilson (National Museum of American Art, Smithsonian Institution, Washington, D.C., Museum purchase, Catherine Walden Myer Fund); Alexander Hamilton (National Gallery of Art, Smithsonian Institution, Washington, D.C., Gift of the Avalon Foundation, 1952); George Washington (The New-York Historical Society); Alexander Hamilton (National Gallery of Art, Smithsonian Institution, Washington, D.C., Gift of the Avalon Foundation, 1952); James Madison (Colonial Williamsburg Foundation); George Washington (The New-York Historical Society); James Madison (Colonial Williamsburg Foundation); Benjamin Franklin, detail (National Portrait Gallery, Smithsonian Institution, Washington, D.C.); George Washington (The New-York Historical Society); Thomas Jefferson (Maryland Historical Society); John Jay (The New-York Historical Society); Alexander Hamilton (National Gallery of Art, Smithsonian Institution, Washington, D.C., Gift of the Avalon Foundation, 1952); Thomas Jefferson (Maryland Historical Society); John Marshall (Collection of the Supreme Court of the United States, Washington, D.C.); Thomas Jefferson (Maryland Historical Society); John Marshall (Collection of the Supreme Court of the United States, Washington, D.C.); Daniel Webster (Hood Museum of Art, Dartmouth College, Hanover, N.H., Gift of Dr. George C. Shattuck, Class of 1803); Andrew Jackson, detail (National Portrait Gallery, Smithsonian Institution, Washington, D.C.); James Madison, detail (National Portrait Gallery, Smithsonian Institution, Washington, D.C.); Alexis de Tocqueville (The Granger Collection, New York); Roger B. Taney (Collection of the Supreme Court of the United States, Washington, D.C.); John Quincy Adams, detail (National Portrait Gallery, Smithsonian Institution, Washington, D.C.); Henry Clay, detail (National Portrait Gallery, Smithsonian Institution, Washington, D.C.); Abraham Lincoln (National Archives, Washington, D.C.); Abraham Lincoln (National Archives, Washington, D.C.); David Davis (Illinois State Historical Library, Old State Capitol, Springfield, Illinois); Andrew Johnson (National Archives, Washington, D.C.); Susan B. Anthony, detail (National Portrait Gallery, Smithsonian Institution, Washington, D.C.), Morrison R. Waite (Collection of the Supreme Court of the United States, Washington, D.C.); John Marshall Harlan (Collection of the Supreme Court of the United States, Washington, D.C.), William Gladstone (National Portrait Gallery, London); John Marshall Harlan (Collection of the Supreme Court of the United States, Washington, D.C.); John Marshall Harlan (Collection of the Supreme Court of the United States, Washington, D.C); Oliver Wendell Holmes (AP/Wide World Photos); Charles Evans Hughes (Collection of the Supreme Court of the United States, Washington, D.C.); Oliver Wendell Holmes (AP/Wide World Photos); Oliver Wendell Holmes (AP/Wide World Photos); Oliver Wendell Holmes (AP/Wide World Photos); Clarence Darrow (Chicago Historical Society); William Howard Taft (Collection of the Supreme Court of the United States, Washington, D.C.); Louis D. Brandeis (Collection of the Supreme Court of the United States, Washington, D.C.); Louis D. Brandeis (Collection of the Supreme Court of the United States, Washington, D.C.); Charles Evans Hughes (Collection of the Supreme Court of the United States, Washington, D.C.); Louis D. Brandeis (Collection of the Supreme Court of the United States, Washington, D.C.); George Sutherland (Collection of the Supreme Court of the United States, Washington, D.C.); Owen J. Roberts (Collection of the Supreme Court of the United States, Washington, D.C.); James R. McReynolds (Collection of the Supreme Court of the United States, Washington, D.C.); Harlan Fiske Stone (Collection of the Supreme Court of the United States, Washington, D.C.); Benjamin N. Cardozo (Collection of the Supreme Court of the United States, Washington, D.C.); Charles Evans Hughes (Collection of the Supreme Court of the United States, Washington, D.C.); Franklin D. Roosevelt, detail (National Portrait Gallery, Smithsonian Institution, Washington, D.C.); Robert H. Jackson (Collection of the Supreme Court of the United States, Washington, D.C.); Hugo L. Black (UPI/Bettmann Newsphotos); Robert H. Jackson (Collection of the Supreme Court of the United States, Washington, D.C.); Felix Frankfurter (UPI/Bettmann Newsphotos); Earl Warren (UPI/Bettmann Newsphotos); Harry S Truman (AP/Wide World Photos); Hugo L. Black (UPI/Bettmann Newsphotos); J. William Fulbright (AP/Wide World Photos); William J. Brennan, Jr. (Collection of the Supreme Court of the United States, Washington, D.C.); Earl Warren (UPI/Bettmann Newsphotos); Earl Warren (UPI/Bettmann Newsphotos); Lewis F. Powell, Jr. (Collection of the Supreme Court of the United States, Washington, D.C.); William O. Douglas (Collection of the Supreme Court of the United States, Washington, D.C.); Warren E. Burger (Collection of the Supreme Court of the United States, Washington, D.C.); William J. Brennan, Jr. (Collection of the Supreme Court of the United States, Washington, D.C.)